55852.
C18s

WORLD HISTORY

Classical Civilization:
India

WORLD HISTORY

WORLD HISTORY: CLASSICAL CIVILIZATION: INDIA
Copyright © 2013 by Morgan Reynolds Publishing

All rights reserved
This book, or parts thereof, may not be reproduced
in any form except by written consent of the publisher.
For more information write:
Morgan Reynolds Publishing, Inc.
620 South Elm Street, Suite 387
Greensboro, NC 27406 USA

Library of Congress Cataloging-in-Publication Data

Cunningham, Kevin, 1966-
Classical civilization. India / by Kevin Cunningham.
    p. cm. -- (World history)
Includes bibliographical references and index.
ISBN 978-1-59935-175-9 -- ISBN 978-1-59935-304-3 (e-book) 1. Indus
civilization--Juvenile literature. I. Title. II. Title: India.
DS425.C86 2014
934--dc23
                                   2012035351

PRINTED IN THE UNITED STATES OF AMERICA
First Edition

Book cover and interior designed by:
Ed Morgan, navyblue design studio
Greensboro, NC

WORLD
HISTORY

CLASSICAL CIVILIZATION:
INDIA

Kevin Cunningham

MORGAN
REYNOLDS
PUBLISHING

GREENSBORO, NORTH CAROLINA

Contents

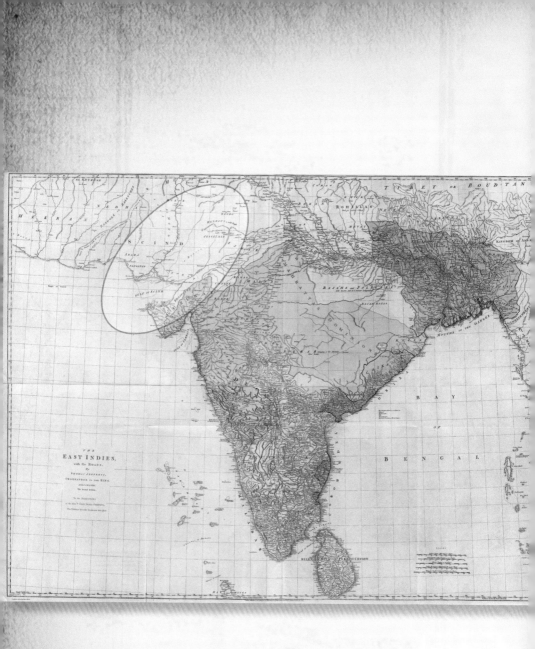

A vintage map of the East Indies by Thomas Jefferys, geographer to King George III. Ancient Greece with the Indus River Valley area is highlighted.

Chapter One:
Ancient Cities

The once-common version of ancient history held that
sophisticated social, economic, religious, and technological
societies began with the so-called cradle civilizations of
Mesopotamia, along the Tigris and Euphrates Rivers, and
in Egypt, on the banks of the Nile. Modern archaeology
has broadened that view. Excavations around the world
have since uncovered evidence of very ancient civilizations
in places as far apart as China's Yellow River and in
coastal Peru.

Starting in the 1800s, archaeologists began to
investigate ruins in the valley of the Indus River, in
what is modern-day Pakistan but was then part of India.
Archaeologists digging into the ancient cities in the mid-
1800s had no idea they had discovered a sophisticated
culture. They assumed no cities existed in ancient India.

Work at the sites intensified in the 1920s. The later generations of archaeologists found the Indus Valley cities were as old as those of Mesopotamia and Egypt—and part of a civilization larger in area than either of the fabled cradle civilizations.

Out of the Past

At its peak, the Indus Valley Civilization (IVC) was probably the largest organized society on earth. The hundreds of cities and settlements attributed to the IVC stretched from a region around Lothal, a site in India's Gujarat state, west along the coast of the Arabian Sea to Sutkagen Dor, near the modern-day border of Pakistan and Iran. From the coast the IVC covered the area up the Indus and some of its tributaries almost as far as the Himalaya Mountains. Scattered settlements reached west into Afghanistan. Others dotted the landscape east beyond today's New Delhi.

The IVC's size is not its only unusual feature. Its cities and towns seem to have been connected to one-another, whereas other civilizations of the time existed as a series of independent city-states.

Details about the IVC's origins and the civilization itself remain scarce. Archaeological work is a slow business, and archaeologists have only really known about the IVC since the 1920s. The bulk of work done on the sites did not begin until the 1980s.

Nonetheless, studies of ruins and artifacts by experts across several fields have filled in some of the blank spots. Much of the information has come from digs at two major cities: Harappa, on the Ravi River, and Mohenjo-daro, on the Indus.

Early Years at Harappa

Archaeologists sometimes refer to the IVC as the Harappan civilization, after the major archaeological site at modern-day Harappa, Pakistan. Work at Harappa suggests people lived in the area since Neolithic times. Around 3300 BCE, the pre-Harappan people began to organize into a sedentary culture. Archaeologists sometimes describe the time period as the Ravi Phase, after the nearby river. Harappa's ancient builders constructed the earliest version of the town on a pair of low hills, probably for protection from floods. People lived in huts with reed walls built on a frame of wooden posts.

The pre-Harappan society, like that of most of the ancient civilizations, developed in a dry region. River valleys, watered in part by spring floods, provided fertile cropland. But the Indus Valley region lacked good building material like limestone. The dry climate also limited the growth of forests that could have provided wood.

The pre-Harappans adapted by learning to heat bricks, first in the sunlight and later in kilns (ovens). Brick remained

The Indus River near Leh, the largest town in the Ladakh district of India. Leh was an important stopover on the trade route along the Indus Valley between Tibet to the east, Kashmir to the west, and also between India and China for centuries.

the primary building material as the Harappan civilization expanded. The sun-dried, easier-to-make mud bricks remained common in small towns. Higher quality kiln-fired brick, once invented, dominated in the larger cities.

European archaeologists initially doubted that the pre-Harappans could come up with the idea of towns on their own. Since no one had found evidence of earlier Bronze or Stone Age settlements, it seemed to archaeologists that the pre-Harappans appeared from thin air. Human societies simply do not form that way. Some experts suggested the ancient Indians must have adopted ideas from Mesopotamia.

Archaeological work eventually turned up the Bronze and Stone Age evidence. Experts, now able to draw a line from prehistoric hunters and gatherers to ancient city builders, agree the ancient Indians did not borrow their ideas from the Near East—and did not have to.

Growth and Expansion

Around 2600 BCE, the Indus Valley peoples entered what archaeologists call the Early Harappan Phase, an era of increasingly sophisticated technology and organization. The civilization soon progressed to a more advanced Mature Phase that lasted until 1900 BCE. In some areas the transformation from pre-Harappan to Early Harappan took place later than 2600 BCE.

By that date Harappa itself was a large town and entering its greatest age. From roughly 2600 to 1900 BCE, Harappa spread into a large city by taking over more of the area hills. Farmers and others used most or all of the available land nearby. A brick wall protected at least part of the city. Cities of comparable size, as yet unexplored by archaeologists, appeared elsewhere in the valleys of the Indus and other nearby rivers.

Mound of Dead Men

Located in Sindh province in Pakistan, Mohenjo-daro—
The Mound of Dead Men—appeared around 2600 BCE.
Mohenjo-daro sat between two river valleys. The Indus itself
flowed to the west. A now-dry river, the Ghaggar-Hakra,
lay to the east. Since rivers provided the main avenues of
transportation, Mohenjo-daro commanded two important
trading routes. Control of trade added to the city's wealth
and helped make it into one of the largest Indus Valley cities.

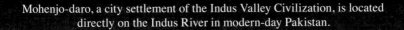

Mohenjo-daro, a city settlement of the Indus Valley Civilization, is located
directly on the Indus River in modern-day Pakistan.

Mohenjo-daro was built on a plateau to avoid flooding. Over hundreds of years, townspeople concerned with floodwaters constructed more buildings atop mud brick platforms. The largest platforms rose thirty-nine feet (twelve meters) over today's plain.

Though cities were important, the majority of people inhabiting the Indus Valley lived in rural areas. Farmers found the fertile soil of the river valleys good for crops like wheat, rice, dates, mustard, and cotton. Agriculture benefited further from the work, fertilizer, and products provided by domestic animals. People kept sheep, pigs, goats, and dogs. Ancient Indians probably domesticated the chicken, one of the modern world's most important food animals, though it seems they had more interest in betting on cockfights than in eggs or drumsticks. Water buffalo and zebu (a species of cattle) pulled plows and carts.

Both fishermen and traders lived along the rivers that provided their livelihoods. Further out, wilderness areas provided game and wild plants.

All of a Kind

Mud brick had limits. Rain, wind, and other natural forces wore down the bricks. Furthermore, bricks had to be small to keep their strength, unlike stone, which could be cut in huge, sturdy blocks. These factors caused mud brick structures to buckle over time and may have been the reason Indus Valley peoples did not build pyramids or the other huge structures found in Egypt and Mesopotamia. In fact, the lack of such buildings lulled early archaeologists into dismissing Harappa as unimportant.

Later investigators turned up details that made it clear IVC towns were in their way as exceptional as towers or pyramids.

Builders throughout the Harappan civilization used standardized bricks, that is, bricks of similar length, width, and depth. Standardization is so common in

today's societies that we take for granted that 10,000 nails or athletic shoes will all be the same. But standardized anything was rare in early societies that lacked iron tools, let alone machines. Indus Valley brick was of high enough quality to fool those who first studied the ruins into thinking the brick was modern. Workers in the 1800s used thousands-year-old Harappan bricks on a nearby railroad.

People in the Indus Valley believed in standardization on a large scale, too. Archaeologists were surprised to find that towns throughout the IVC had layouts that in most ways matched Harappa and Mahenjo-daro. No other early civilization laid out entire cities and towns according to a plan, let alone built dozens of towns with more or less the same layout. It would be thousands of years before pre-planned towns became widespread again in India.

Grids and Great Baths

A typical IVC town had two parts. The first, the so-called citadel, was built on a raised brick platform. The citadel area included a town's better built and more luxurious structures, assuming it had any of the latter. Harappa's citadel may have been fifty feet (15.24 meters) tall.

To the east of the citadel lay a lower town where most of the people lived. Planners laid out the lower town on a grid system, with streets running north-south and east-west. Regular streets were twice as wide as smaller side lanes. Major roads were one-and-a-half or two times as wide as streets. These ratios, like the grid, were common across the IVC, though features like deserts or seacoasts forced some towns to partially alter the layout.

Wide streets and roads allowed ox-drawn carts to pass. Yoking animals to pull carts may have been another Indian invention—people in ancient India may have used the wheel for transportation before anyone else. Wells were placed throughout a city to provide drinking water for animals and people.

City plans also included waste disposal. Ducts covered with brick carried sewage from homes to similar, larger mains beneath the streets.

Archaeologists are still working to figure out the different kinds of buildings. As expected, though, the lower towns were full of houses. The floor plans are familiar even to the modern eye. Many houses appear to have had walled courtyards. Each house had a latrine (bathroom) connected to the sewer system. Brick's limits probably kept most or all of the homes to one or two stories.

One unique aspect of the houses is the attached bathing areas or bathhouses. Cities, too, seem to have provided large bathhouses. In fact, the only building positively identified by archaeologists is a bath house at Mohenjo-daro. The Great Bath, as it is called, stretches about thirty-nine feet (twelve meters) long and twenty-two feet (seven meters) wide. The deepest part is almost eight feet (two-and-a-half meters) deep. A shallow ledge runs down one side. Staircases, one on the north end and another on the south, led into the water.

The local builders water-proofed the bath's floor and sides by fitting together bricks and sealing them with a kind of plaster. A layer of tar on each side and perhaps under the floor prevented leaks. The building around the bath contained a well for drawing water—for the bath or not, we don't know—and doors on three sides. Some experts think townspeople used the bath in religious ceremonies. But it remains unclear how (or who, or what) they worshipped. It's not even certain religion played a part at all.

Near the Great Bath is another large area marked off by brick. Earlier generations of archaeologists, believing such a large structure might have stored grain, nicknamed it the Granary. But there's no evidence it held grain. More and more experts prefer to call it the Great Hall, though it was possibly a government building, temple, or something else.

Top: Remains of an ancient yet sophisticated sewage system at Lothal, a famous port city now far from the ocean. Each house in Lothal had toilets, which were linked with drains covered with burnt clay bricks.
Bottom: Excavated ruins of Mohenjo-daro, with the Great Bath in the front.

Walls eventually became a city feature. Digs have unearthed parts of a wall up to thirteen feet thick at Harappa. Walls around the citadel had a base forty feet thick and probably were meant to hold off floods as much as hostile invaders.

Smaller walls inside Mohenjo-daro's lower town suggest some people lived within walled neighborhoods on top of mounds. Possibly each neighborhood was home to certain types of craftsmen—pottery makers here, tool makers there—or open only to people of a certain social class.

Mysterious Seals

Archaeologists have found hundreds of small seals across the IVC lands. Many are squarish or rectangular and a few centimeters wide and long. Some have a hole for a string or cord that allowed people to wear the seal. Most seals were made of steatite (also called soapstone) and usually feature an image, or images. Often the image is of an animal— tiger, elephant, bull, buffalo, rhinoceros. The most popular image is of an unusual creature that seems to have a horned horse or zebra head atop a bull's body. The creature, nicknamed the unicorn, appears on hundreds of the seals.

In many cases a seal features up to five symbols in an unknown language used across the Indus Valley culture. The symbols are pictographs, not letters. The writing system is very old. Traces of it appear on pieces of Ravi Phase pottery dating to almost 5,000 years ago.

Archaeologists have found about four hundred pictographs. Human experts and computer codebreaking technology have failed to unlock the language. If deciphered, the writing system may offer many details of daily life, customs, economy, and religion. It may even give names to a few individuals—we don't know the identity of a single person who lived in the IVC.

With the Harappan language still locked, we cannot be sure how people used the seals. But the consensus today is

Hundreds of tiny soapstone seals like the ones pictured here have been found in the architectural ruins of Indus Valley cities. It is believed that the seals were used to mark property in merchant trade, like a signet ring. The majority of seals portray male animals with horns.

that the information conveyed by the image-text combination most likely had to do with trade. Clues hint that at least some seals had value. It seems the authorities restricted access to seal manufacturing areas. That custom—perhaps it was a law—parallels how modern governments limit access to facilities that print money.

Indus Valley Art

Crafts in the pre-Harappan era included the manufacturing of pottery and tools. Craftsmen turned stones like agate and lapis lazuli into beads. Others used fabric to press patterns onto terracotta beads, or colored soapstone beads with heat and glazes. Archaeologists have also found many kinds of jewelry.

As time passed, craftsmen developed more skills. Terracotta pots improved in quality with better furnaces. Many pieces had geometric shapes or animal figures painted on them. Copper and bronze tools—razors, pots, pans—and fixtures like mirrors became more common. Jewelry-makers fashioned bangles and other items from ivory, seashells, and semiprecious stones.

IVC artists may have also practiced sculpture. Digs have unearthed small figurines at a few sites. It's possible some or all came from other regions through trade—opinions are mixed. But experts lean toward crediting an Indus Valley artist with the creation of the famous dancing girl figurine found at Mohenjo-daro. Made of bronze and standing 4.25 inches (10.8 centimeters) high, the dancing girl is actually not dancing. Instead she's striking a haughty pose, her chin up, one hand on her hip, her nude body adorned with a necklace and bangles.

This "Dancing Girl" statue was found in a house in Mohenjo-daro in 1926.

This stone head, known as the Priest-King, shows a man
with a beard, wearing a ribbon headband. His robe, or
cloak, has a three-leaf pattern on it.

Another sculpture, the Priest-King, was discovered at
Mohenjo-daro in 1927. No one knows if the steatite figure
really represents a priest or a king. No one even knows for
sure that priests and kings ruled in the Indus Valley. But
the man's headband, decorated cloak, and proud expression
give off an air of authority, and the title seemed to fit.

IVC artists produced less refined items, too. Toys, some
with wheels, have been discovered. So have terracotta and
bronze figurines of women with large ears or headdresses,
strange faces, and skirts. Some experts have proposed the
figurines represent goddesses. But as with so much else, no
one knows for sure.

Studying the Dead

Close to one hundred skeletons unearthed at a Harappa cemetery have provided important information about who lived in the city. The bones have genetic traits matching Mediterranean peoples as well as Proto-Austroloid peoples found today from India to the native populations of Australia. Tests indicate the dead Harappans had an average lifespan of about thirty years. Five feet, nine inches would have been considered tall. Most of the bodies were buried with their heads pointing north. Jewelry decorated some bodies. A number of coffins rested in brick chambers.

Late Phase

Around 2000 BCE, the Harappan civilization began to decline. Cities ceased to use the grid pattern for streets. Drainage systems failed. The quality of pottery and other manufactured goods fell off. In Harappa, houses became smaller. Later the Harappans abandoned them—perhaps quickly.

The reasons why, like so much else, remain a mystery. For a long time, experts thought invaders from Central Asia called the Arya, or Aryans, destroyed the Indus Valley cities. The idea still appears in textbooks and documentaries. But most scholars today dismiss the idea.

"Despite extensive excavations at the largest Harappan sites," said George F. Dales, an archaeologist of IVC sites and founder of the Harappa Archeological Research Project, "there is not a single bit of evidence that can be brought forth as unconditional proof of an armed conquest . . . on the scale of the supposed Aryan invasion."

Some experts think a change in environment—possibly with natural disasters involved—may have played a role. Clues suggest changes in the Indus River system took place around the time decline set in. In some places rivers may have dried up. At Mohenjo-daro, it is possible the Indus switched course and began to flood inhabited areas. The river system provided both water for agriculture and waterways for transporting goods.

Change the flow of water, and many towns would have found it harder to grow food or make money. Either could cause major problems for a society.

As with so much about the Harappan civilization, however, there's little evidence any of that actually happened. There are experts who doubt changes in the river system would alone cause the collapse of a large, well-organized civilization. Whatever happened, by about 1700 BCE—the date moves according to new findings—the IVC had entered its last decades.

Nothing replaced the organized empire that had grown and thrived throughout the Indus Valley. But the culture that built Harappa and Mohenjo-daro did not vanish, either. People carried parts of it with them as they fragmented into smaller communities or migrated to new areas. The Harappan civilization, even when long gone, influenced India's history.

Comparative Timeline of Ancient Civilizations [all dates approximate]

3100s BCE
India: Indus Valley Civilization, early phase
Mesopotamia: Writing and cities

2500s BCE
India: Indus Valley Civilization, mature phase
Egypt: Pyramid at Giza built

1500s BCE
India: Earliest Arya migrants enter India
Mesoamerica: Olmec cities appear

800s BCE
India: Vedic era
Mediterranean: Phoenician culture dominates

300s BCE
India: Maurya Empire begins
Greece: Alexander the Great enters India

0 CE
India: Roman fleets sailing to Malabar Coast
China: First census by the Han Dynasty

Chapter Two:
Words Spoken, Words Written

According to SIL International, Indians today speak almost 440 languages, plus hundreds of dialects of those languages. India's linguistic diversity has widely varied roots, some that date from a few centuries ago—as with the widespread use of English—and some going back to prehistory—as with the Dravidian languages spoken in the country's south. A significant part of India's religious and cultural heritage grew out of the use of Vedic Sanskrit, an ancient language brought from outside India by a people still wrapped in myth and mystery.

Horse People

Around 1500 BCE—perhaps later, probably not earlier—waves of nomadic tribes began to enter northwest India from what is modern-day Iran. In their written works, created much later, these peoples called themselves *arya*, or noble. Arya, however, was an adjective, rather than an ethnic label like German or Chinese. Historians in need

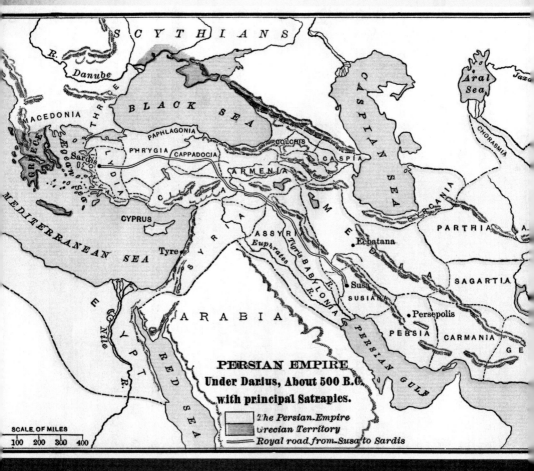

A nineteenth century lithograph of the Persian Empire about 500 BCE

of an ethnic term often refer to these peoples as Indo-Aryans or Aryans, as well as Arya or arya. (Note: Aryan in this context bears no relationship to the term used in Nazi Germany or by modern neo-Nazis for an alleged master race.)

The Arya were probably seminomadic. Living in family or tribal units, the men rode horses to maintain large cattle herds. It appears the Arya had also mastered the chariot, a technology developed in Central Asia centuries earlier.

Cattle played a central role in Arya life. In addition to providing meat and other products, cattle measured wealth. Relatedly, they served as currency. An Arya bought goods and services for this many or that many cows. Tribal warfare for cows, and therefore wealth, probably kept Arya males busy. Linguistic study suggests the Arya did not grow crops. The ancient language the horsemen carried into India lacks words common to any farmer's vocabulary.

For years historians painted the Arya as bloodthirsty invaders. Histories laid the subjugation of Indian peoples, even the destruction of the Indus Valley Civilization, on mounted Arya warriors. That version still gets repeated. But modern historians generally accept the Arya did not invade as much as migrate into India over a period of time. How they treated the Indians they encountered remains unclear. No records date from the time of contact.

Historians parse out hints from Vedic Sanskrit texts written centuries later and put down not as histories but as religious texts that celebrated Arya beliefs and culture. The texts suggest the Arya looked down on India's peoples. They called them barbarian (*dasyu*) and slave (*dasa*) and at times made war against them. Conquerors tend to impose their culture on those they defeat, and it's likely the Arya were no different. Ancient laws forbade the intermarriage of Arya and native Indians they saw as inferiors. The Arya also made a particular effort to keep their language free of Indian influences.

27

The effort worked, to some extent, with their religious speech. But non-Sanskrit words found a way into everyday spoken language. The Arya had no choice but to adopt Indian terms. As they traveled farther and farther into India, they continually came across things unknown to them, like elephants and rice. Lacking a word of their own for these things, they borrowed a local term from the people around them.

Vedic and Sanskrit

Linguists and historians refer to the Arya's original ancient language as Vedic, Vedic Sanskrit, or Old Indo-Aryan. Most of the languages spoken today in northern and north-central India—areas settled by the Arya—evolved from Vedic.

The term *Vedic* comes from four collections of hymns, prayers, and other religious writings known as the Vedas. The Vedas began as entirely oral texts, with the contents taught by one generation to the next. It must have involved painstaking lessons. The priests, or Brahmins, in charge of using and passing on the knowledge in the Vedas believed their gods would listen only if the hymns and prayers were recited perfectly—without change in words, tone, rhythm, or any other element. Experts think the need for exactitude helped Vedic Sanskrit resist errors or change. Thus, the language remained in a state the elite Brahmins considered pure for century after century.

The *Rig Veda* is the most ancient of the Vedas. The earliest parts of the text, dating to about 1500 BCE, rank among the world's oldest religious writings. At the same time, linguists consider the Vedic Sanskrit used in the *Rig Veda* one of the most ancient members of the Indo-European language family. (The hundreds of modern Indo-European languages and dialects dominate modern Europe, the Western Hemisphere, and Central and South Asia. They include English, Spanish, and Hindi.) Later writers added to the *Rig Veda* over several centuries. The text eventually reached 1028 hymns.

An early nineteenth century *Rig Veda* in Sanskrit on paper. The *Rig Veda*, the earliest of the Vedic hymns, is one of the world's oldest books.

The *Rig Veda*, like all the Vedas, remains relevant today as a Hindu religious text. It also offers historians glimpses into the everyday life, belief, and customs of the Arya, portraying their early culture as tribal and warlike, with mastery of lands but undefined borders.

Three other Vedas—the *Sama*, *Yajur*, and *Atharva*—come out of a later period, from 1000 to 600 BCE. By the time of the later Vedas, the Arya had migrated and conquered farther north, south, and east. The Arya, having spread into Northern India, threw off their ancient system of tribes and rajas (leaders in war) in favor of societies with nobles who ruled kingdoms with defined, though often changing, territories. Historians use the term *Aryanization* to describe the imposition of Arya culture on native Indian peoples. The process continued for centuries. Indeed, it continues into the present day, as northern India's dominant Aryanized culture continues to find its way into once-isolated traditional societies in rain forests and the Himalayas.

Starting in approximately 900 BCE, religious schools began to compose new oral texts called the *Brahmanas*. The Brahmanas explained the background and meanings of sacred rituals laid out in the Vedas, as well as giving instructions on how to perform the rituals. A Brahmana always commented on one of the four Vedas. We have no idea how many were created. Nineteen whole Brahmanas survived to today. Fragments of others—some massive, others no more than a page—also remain.

Early Vedic literature features gods, heroes, and other divine beings central to both the Hindu faith and Indian culture. The *Rig Veda* mentions one of the most beloved ancient stories, that of the king Pururavas and his great love, the divine water nymph Urvashi (sometimes called Usas). Essentially a love poem, the Pururavas passages tell how the king spent four autumns with Urvashi. When Pururavas unwittingly breaks a rule regarding their marriage, Urvashi leaves him. Nothing he says can bring her back. Vedic-era Brahmins used the story to guide users through certain rituals. But the tale's beautiful poetry and theme of tragic romance inspired storytellers ever after.

The Vedas and Brahmanas, while important, form only the base of India's vast ancient literature. Most of that literature was first created, like the Vedas, in purely oral form, since the Arya and their earliest descendants did not use writing. Furthermore, it was meant to be performed, rather than read, by the Brahmins. The favor of the gods rode on proper performance as well as perfect recitation.

The Upanishads and Beyond

Texts known as the Upanishads grew out of the Brahmanas and represent the last of the old Vedic oral texts. Hindus keep them at the core of their religious teachings. Scholars across many disciplines accept the Upanishads as masterpieces of literature and philosophy as well as important sacred works. The Sanskrit words of the syllables in *Upanishad* mean "sit down near to," i.e., as one does to listen to a teacher or spiritual leader.

Pururavas, as depicted in the 1914 book *Myths of the Hindus & Buddhists*

Opinions vary, but generally experts recognize between ten and thirteen core Upanishads. Almost two hundred so-called minor Upanishads have been added over the centuries. Priests made many contributions, not surprisingly. But so did poets and sages.

To state things in a very simplified way, the Upanishads explore the relationship—and ultimate oneness—between the divine, or the All, called Brahman, and the perfect spirit, or Atman, of each living thing. Ideas from the Upanishads— karma (action), samsara (reincarnation, or rebirth) and moksha (nirvana, a state of escape from rebirth) to name three—have become familiar around the world. So have meditation and yoga. These two practices, both discussed in the texts, are ways to pursue the union of one's Atman with the All.

The Upanishads took many forms. Some employed verse to teach. Others used conversations. Book Seven of *Chandogya*, for example, has a teacher instructing a curious student. Each chapter ends with the latter asking if there is anything greater than whatever concept is under discussion in the chapter. The instructor replies that there is. Will you please tell me what it is?, the student replies. The next book then begins with the teacher explaining, and ends with the same back-and-forth. Constructing a lesson in that way created a rhythm that made it easy for listeners to follow.

From Living Speech to Second Language

Indian society, influenced by the Arya, stratified into a caste system. Castes represented layers of society, from the Aryanized elite through levels that dictated one's work as well as one's place in the social order, to a lowest caste of "untouchables." The caste system forbade marrying or working outside one's caste. The Brahman (later Hindu) religion reinforced these rules by preaching acceptance of one's caste and of living within caste limits.

By the 600s BCE, the old Vedic Sanskrit had become what linguists call simply Sanskrit. Though the spoken language of the elite—nobles, Brahmins, and the learned— Sanskrit as a spoken tongue already had been eclipsed throughout most of India's Aryanized regions. Members of other castes spoke *Prakrits*, local Indo-European native languages influenced by, but no longer, Sanskrit. The process continued for many centuries, adding to India's linguistic diversity.

Even as spoken Sanskrit faded, India's literature explored new directions.

In the sixth century BCE, two philosophical systems, Buddhism and Jainism, rose to challenge Brahminism. Buddhism and Jainism merged new interpretations of the world with ideas borrowed from older systems of belief.

Organized by men of noble birth—Siddharta Gautama and Mahavira, respectively—and rejecting Brahmin ideas like caste and wasteful ritual sacrifice, Buddhism and Jainism appealed greatly to lower-class Indians on the losing end of the caste system. Believers in the new philosophies further rejected Brahmin ideas by initially using their local Prakrit vernaculars rather than Sanskrit to spread Buddhist and Jainist ideas.

Sanskrit writers, meanwhile, turned to creating epic poetry. Two works are considered supreme: the *Mahabharata* and the *Ramayana*.

A 1470 sculpture of Mahavira, the spiritual leader of Jainism

Age of Epics

The *Mahabharata* runs to almost 1.8 million words. It is the world's longest poem. Admirers worldwide consider it a masterpiece of world literature. Though attributed to Vyasa, a being in Hindu tradition, experts believe no single person composed the entire work. Researchers have determined the poem began with a small core that later writers expanded upon at enormous length.

The work concerns the conflict between two related families. The exiled Pandavas and their kin the Kauravas each have a claim on the throne of a powerful kingdom. The sides fail to make peace with one-another and go to war. The *Bhagavad-Gita*, a work within the larger work, portrays how Arjura, an indomitable Pandava warrior-prince, hesitates to attack when he sees beloved relatives in the Kauravas ranks. He turns to his chariot driver, the divine being Krishna (at that moment disguised as a mortal) for advice:

> Krishna, I hanker not for victory,
> Nor for the kingdom, nor yet for things of pleasure.
> What use to us a kingdom, friend,
> What use enjoyment or life [itself]?
>
> Those for whose sake we covet
> Kingdom, delights and things of pleasure,
> Here stand they, arrayed for battle,
> Surrendering both wealth and life.

Krishna replies that duty demands that Arjura attack. To defeat the Kauravas would uphold righteousness, and the upholding of righteousness, regardless of the personal pain or cost, takes precedence over anything else. His words—and his dramatic revelation of himself as the earthly form of a god—convince Arjura to do his duty.

34

Arjuna meets Krishna, as depicted in the undated book *Mahabharata*.

An eleventh century lintel, or architectural design, representing
an episode of the *Ramayana*

The *Mahabharata* dramatizes conflicts between characters and conflicts within the characters over duty, right and wrong, and other issues. When the Pandavas win out, they go on to conquer an empire. Yet the triumph is temporary. In old age, they give up their worldly power and goods. All but one dies while climbing the Himalayas to reach heaven.

The *Bhagavad Gita* is a sacred text of Hinduism and an ongoing influence in modern Indian culture. Mohandas Gandhi returned to the work throughout his life for inspiration and hope, said it had the greatest influence on his thought, and called it his spiritual dictionary. It is also the best known of ancient India's literary works outside of India. Figures as diverse as Henry David Thoreau and Albert Einstein admired it. Physicist Robert Oppenheimer thought of one of Krishna's awe-inspiring declarations ("Now, I am become Death, the destroyer of worlds") upon seeing the first atomic bomb test.

The second major epic of the period, the *Ramayana*, follows the life of the hero Rama. Indian tradition ascribes authorship of most of the *Ramayana* to Valmiki, considered to be India's first poet, with added material tacked on by others.

Rama, like Arjura an exile, wins the hand of the princess Sita through heroic deeds. When the demon king Ravana abducts Sita, Rama—accompanied by his brother and the monkey warrior Hanuman—tracks Ravana to the demon's island city. There Rama's armies confront and defeat Ravana's forces, and Rama destroys the demon king. A final book, believed to be a late addition, deals with Rama's kingship and troubled marriage, and his eventual ascension to the heavens.

Works in dance, theater, song, sculpture and other visual art, written and oral literature, and architecture owe their inspiration to the *Ramayana*. Different versions, usually in local languages, became popular in various parts of India. The Buddhists and Jains created their own Ramayanas.

The epic also traveled with the spread of Hindu culture throughout South Asia. From the early centuries CE, written, sung, and danced Ramayanas appeared from Tibet to the Philippines. Thailand's version, the *Ramakien*, is one of the epics of the country's literature. The Rama story in all its forms remains popular today. Just recently, new *Ramayana*-based novels, films, graphic novels, and plays have appeared. People from around the world flock to the Indian city of Varanasi to see a version of the story reenacted over the course of an entire week.

Beloved of the Gods

Sanskrit, as a purely oral language, had no written script of its own. But Prakrit-speakers created a script called Brahmi to write in their tongues, and Brahmi eventually was used for Sanskrit. Surviving examples of languages in Brahmi script represent some of India's earliest known writing. Some of these early examples, however, do not exist in books, but on stone, including remarkable monuments raised at the command of an ancient emperor.

His name was Ashoka. He belonged to a dynasty Buddhist and Jain writers named the Maurya. Ashoka's grandfather, the mostly unknown Chandragupta, seems to have risen from humble origins to conquer much of northern and central India. In time the Maurya Empire covered lands from the Bay of Bengal to the east to the Arabian Sea on the west, and north to include most of Afghanistan.

According to legend, Chandragupta gave up the throne, embraced Jainism, and then followed Jain teachings by starving himself to death. His son Bindusara ruled next. What little we know of the time suggests Ashoka was not Bindusara's heir but one son out of many. Around 268 BCE Ashoka won the throne. Seven or eight years later, he set out on a campaign that expanded the Maurya Empire—and changed Ashoka's life.

The Maurya armies marched on Kalinga, a large central Indian nation on the Bay of Bengal. According to Ashoka's own account, hundreds of thousands of people died during or after the war. Ashoka exiled 150,000 more. Some historians dispute the figures. Ancient accounts, regardless of culture, are notorious for inflating army sizes and body counts. But whatever the numbers, the Kalinga bloodbath had an extraordinary effect on Ashoka. The victorious emperor rejected war and conquest in favor of Buddhist nonviolence.

> On conquering Kalinga, the Beloved of the Gods [Ashoka] felt remorse, for, when an independent country is conquered, the slaughter, death and deportation of the people is extremely grievous to the Beloved of the Gods and weighs heavily on his mind. . . . Even those who are fortunate to have escaped, and whose love is undiminished, suffered from the misfortunes of their friends, acquaintances, colleagues and relatives. . . . Today, if a hundredth or a thousandth part of those people who were killed or died or were deported when Kalinga was annexed were to suffer similarly, it would weigh heavily on the mind of the Beloved of the Gods. . . . This inscription of [dharma] has been engraved so that any sons or great-grandsons that I may have should not think of gaining new conquests, and in whatever victories they may gain they should be satisfied with patience and light punishment.

Ashoka went on a pilgrimage, visiting Buddhist sites across his realm. Thereafter he had messages written on large tree leaves and carried to cities to be read to crowds.

In some places, he commanded the message be literally carved in stone.

On caves, and cliff surfaces on highly visible hillsides, and most famously on raised pillars, Ashoka transmitted his beliefs and great works—as well as his expectations—via so-called Rock Edicts: fourteen Major Rock Edicts and seven Pillar Edicts, considered the most important by archaeologists, plus a number of Minor Rock and Pillar Edicts. The quote above comes from the Thirteenth Rock Edict.

A sandstone statue of four lions standing atop a frieze with relief sculptures of other animals topped the pillar at Sarnath, in north-central India. It has since been moved to a local museum. Today the statue, the Lion Capital of Ashoka, serves as India's national emblem. Another capital with four lions stands in Thailand, this one with a Wheel of Law, a Buddhist symbol, shading the beasts.

The Lion Capital of the Emperor Ashoka is the national symbol of India. Carved out of a single block of sandstone, it consists of four lions, back to back, mounted on an abacus, with a frieze in high relief of an elephant, a galloping horse, a bull, and a lion separated by chariot wheels.

Single lions stare out from pillars at a few other sites. An elephant crowns another, a bull yet another.

The Edicts represented Ashoka's declaration that he would govern according to *dharma*, laws that obeyed the ideas of righteous rule and Buddhist-inspired ideas of correct behavior, and encouraged social awareness and tolerance of other peoples and beliefs. "All men are my children," he stated on a Rock Edict at Kalinga.

At the same time, the Edicts exhorted his subjects to obey dharma in their own lives. Though taking the immodest title Devanampiya—Beloved of the Gods—Ashoka nonetheless "spoke" in a straightforward, conversational style, a contrast to the high-sounding pronouncements often heard from history's monarchs. One of Ashoka's attempts to lay out the precepts of dharma said:

> There is no gift comparable to the gift of
> dharma . . . And this is: good behavior toward
> slaves and servants, obedience to mother and
> father, generosity toward friends, acquaintances,
> and relatives . . . and abstention from killing
> living beings.

Ashoka meant to be understood by as many people as possible. In much of India his workers carved his words in Prakrit languages. Areas on the empire's edge received the Edicts in Greek or other scripts popular in those regions. Historians today consider the Rock and Pillar Edicts to be the rough borders of Ashoka's empire, probably the largest in India's history.

Ashoka wanted to encourage dharma, but he still had an empire to run. That required a certain amount of politics. On some Edicts, Ashoka trumpets his works on behalf of the public good, such as planting trees to shade main roads.

Ashoka appointed officials to encourage his subjects to follow the Edicts. True to his vision of dharma and tolerance he allowed many faiths to erect sacred buildings. But he favored Buddhism, and won Buddhist support by lavishing funds on their projects. Thousands of Buddhist temples were built during his reign.

Ashoka's efforts led to an explosion of Buddhist belief within India, but even more so in lands across Asia. He sent Buddhist missionaries far and wide. Tradition claims some reached as far as Egypt.

Sanskrit Masters

India's ancient literature is vast. Post–Vedic era works include texts on grammar, linguistics, law, philosophy, magic, and family, among other topics. By 500 CE, written texts were expanding into areas like engineering, metallurgy, astronomy, medicine, yoga, art, sexuality, mathematics, and even a new board game—chess.

Sanskrit, in the meantime, became a written language when Brahmi provided it with working scripts. Sanskrit held onto its status as the written language of the educated and the elite. Users of Prakrit languages, like Buddhists and Jains, began to copy their sacred texts into Sanskrit.

Sanskrit-language literature entered a golden age in the second century CE. Asvaghosha, a Buddhist convert from North India, became the first Sanskrit dramatist. He also wrote poetry and a widely read biography of the Buddha. The third-century playwright Bhasa set many of his works within the universes of the *Mahabharata* and *Ramayana*.

Kalidasa probably worked in the 300s and 400s, though we know next to nothing about him. Considered by some the greatest literary figure in India's history, Kalidasa reworked classic epics and myths using vivid imagery and soaring language.

His play *The Recognition of Shakuntala* explores a classic Indian plot: the separation and eventual reunion of lovers. A king, Dushyanta, labors on behalf of dharma and order. He falls in love with Shakuntala, a nymph, and they conceive a child. But a curse causes Dushyanta to forget Shakuntala. Only recognizing a ring he had given her can restore his memory. The drama follows the loss of the ring, its eventual discovery, and Dushyanta's search for his beloved when he recovers his memory. Critics and historians often reference *The Recognition of Shakuntala* as a towering work, perhaps the greatest in India's history.

Kalidasa also wrote poetry. His verse epic *Cloud Messenger* contained what is considered some of his best poetry. Another work about separated lovers, *Cloud Messenger* begins with an attendant exiled by his lord to a mountaintop. Seeing a cloud, the attendant asks it to pass on a comforting message to his wife. Much of the poem uses Kalidasa's images to describe the natural wonders the cloud messenger will pass over on its journey to the wife. *Cloud Messenger*, like many of Kalidasa's works, has inspired plays, music, and dances around the world.

Dravidian

Indo-European languages like Sanskrit and the Prakrits, dominant in the north, bumped up against another family of languages in southern India.

The origins of the Dravidian language family that have dominated South India in historic times remain murky, but date back a long time. Early Dravidian languages seem to have evolved beyond the influence of any other known language family. Attempts by linguists to link Dravidian with another family have failed. Dravidian-derived place names in other parts of India, even the north, make it clear that Dravidian cultures at one time existed outside the southern horn of the subcontinent. Some experts suggest Dravidian peoples founded or at least participated in the Indus Valley civilization. This is unproven, however. Nor is it clear when the ancestors of Dravidian peoples migrated into India.

Around 300 BCE, the Tamil began to write in their native Dravidian language, also called Tamil. Brahmi made its way south during Ashoka's time. As it had further north, it provided a script for local languages. Sacred texts in Dravidian languages appear in the record over the next five centuries, as do Tamil epics. Tamil acquired its own script before or during the sixth century CE.

By this time, however, Dravidian had ceased to develop in isolation. Sanskrit words had crept into Dravidian languages. But some linguists believe the real influence went the other way. They find signs of Dravidian grammar and language structure deep within Vedic texts, even the ancient *Rig Veda*.

Today between twenty-three and twenty-eight Dravidian languages are used by approximately 170 million people. Most speakers live in South India and Sri Lanka, with most of the rest in areas of Asia and Africa with large Indian immigrant populations.

Chapter Three:
The Spindle and the Crucible

India's record of technological accomplishment stretches far back into history. The Indus Valley Civilization built on still earlier breakthroughs in engineering, architecture, and agriculture. Though some of that knowledge was lost after the IVC's still-mysterious collapse, the Vedas and later writings in Sanskrit and the Prakrits, as well as outsider accounts, make it clear India was a hotbed of technical and intellectual exploration. Its creations and discoveries have gone on to clothe, feed, teach, entertain, and heal human beings around the world.

The Wool That Grows on Trees

In 1920, archaeologists at Mohenjo-daro discovered pieces of woven cotton stuck to a vase. The Vedas mentioned cotton, but that reference only placed the fabric as far back as (possibly) 1500 BCE. Finding cotton at Mohenjo-daro meant weavers worked it during the earlier Indus Valley Civilization. Archaeologists now believe the tiny pieces of fabric on the vase date to before 2300 BCE, and that it's probable people in the Indus Valley grew and wore cotton earlier.

Many ancient technologies developed in a specific geographic area and spread from there. Cotton was different. Archaeologists credit both India and the Norte Chico culture of coastal Peru—societies separated by thousands of miles, with no hope of contact—with the almost simultaneous domestication of cotton.

Of the four major cotton species used by ancient humans, two evolved in the New World—one in Peru, one in Central America or Mexico—and two in the Old—one in southern Africa, and the one in India.

The Indian cotton species, *Gossypium malavaceae*, grew wild in the Indus Valley. Its pods, called bolls, held grayish

The opening capsule of a cotton plant

cotton balls made up of short strands of lint. Turning stands of cotton into cloth was hard labor. Workers first dug debris out of the lint wads. After combing it out and sorting the strands, they wrapped the cotton yarn around the end of a spinning rod called a spindle. It was then spun using another device called a distaff, an arduous physical chore that wracked the hands, tried one's patience, and required working at a rhythm that kept the strands at a consistent width.

Symbols on Harappan seals make it clear that Indus Valley peoples traded cotton. They measured it out with the same kind of standardized weighing systems IVC traders used to deal in other products.

The Arya found cotton when they migrated into India. It inspired poetic language—the *Rig Veda* compared the universe to a woven cotton fabric. In time, Indian philosophy tied the patience and focus that went into spinning and weaving to meditation practices thought to calm the mind, lift the spirit, and heal the body.

By 1000 BCE cotton had spread into other parts of India. The plant dropped out of written texts for a long time, but historians believe it was one of many products traded with China. The ancient Persians, masters of a sprawling empire centered in parts of modern-day Iran, traded for cotton. As early as 490 BCE, Persian soldiers wore cotton uniforms while warring with Greece. The Greek historian Herodotus mentions fabric from what he called wool-bearing trees in his account of the conflict.

When Alexander the Great and his Greek army arrived in western India in 325 BCE, they quickly tossed off their heavy, hot wool uniforms in favor of local cotton clothes. (Spaniards invading the Inca Empire in the 1500s made the same swap.) Cotton also made handy padding for the hard Greek saddles. When Alexander turned back west, his soldiers took their cotton articles home with them.

The Romans called Indian cotton *carbasina*. In some cases they too used it to clothe soldiers. More often it provided wealthy citizens with a luxury good to covet. Calicut, an Indian city on the Malabar Coast, was well known for its cotton trade, though the cotton itself grew far away. It also produced calico, a durable and cheap cotton fabric.

Weavers in Dhaka, now Bangladesh's capital, first produced *muslin*, an airy fabric that became much desired in places with hot climates.

During the medieval era, Venice, the powerful Italian trading city, imported what little cotton was for sale in Europe. But Europeans outside the Mediterranean seem to have had no desire for the expensive cloth.

It reentered European folklore, however, in the 1300s. The English adventurer John Mandeville wrote an account of his journeys to distant lands. Mandeville claimed cotton—his spelling of the Muslim word *qutun*—came from tiny lambs that lived in pods on plants. His (made-up) tale of the strange animal-plant hybrid endured for five hundred years in Europe, though Indians and Arabs, among others, knew better.

Reinventing Sugar

Humans seemed to have first used sugar about 8,000 years ago in New Guinea. Migrating peoples spread it to South Asia, the Philippines, China, Indonesia, and Pacific islands. The plant then cross bred with related Asian species. These hybrids, sometimes called thin canes, became the sugarcane farmers cultivate today.

For thousands of years, people broke open the grassy sugarcane and either sucked out the sweet liquid or chewed the tissues. It was in India, however, that humans learned to dry out sugar sap in such a way as to get it to form crystals. Crystallizing sugar allowed it to be stored, and thus traded, far outside the plant's home range. The *Atharva Veda* mentioned sugar as a sacrificial offering. References to solid, as opposed to liquid, sugar show up in sixth century BCE writings in India and Persia.

Sugarcane

To get solid sugar, workers began by pressing the cane stalks in a machine to extract the liquid. That done, they boiled the liquid down into crystalized lumps called *khand*. How Indians broke down the liquid into lumpy crystals the Chinese called sand sugar remains partially unclear, but redissolving, recrystalizing, and rewashing the *khand* seems likely. Workers packed the finished sugar into molds that shaped it into loaves for sale.

The Greeks and Romans knew about sugar at least as early as 200 BCE. In the first century CE the Greek physician and traveler Dioscorides noted "a substance called sakkharon, a sort of crystallized honey, in India and Arabia," and claimed that it was good for kidney and bladder problems, as a laxative, and that, if added to water, it could treat cataracts. Indians, meanwhile, used it to treat bowel and digestion problems and to increase the appetite.

India's monopoly on crystalized sugar had ended by the 600s. The Persians had learned to use lime and other agents to separate the white sugar from its natural brown coloring and various impurities. In 647, Indians explained their crystallization technology to a visiting Chinese scientist. He took the technique back to China. Sugar farming boomed in China even as Indians cultivated it less. By the 1500s, ships would put in to Chinese ports to buy sugar for transport to Europe and, ironically, India.

Fabric and Fashion

People in the Indus Valley Civilization used dyes made from plants. At some point, Indians domesticated *Indigofera tinctoria*, or indigo, and extracted from it a blue dye of the same name.

Indigo had great value. Very few plants yielded blue dyes. Over time its cultivation and use spread as far east as Japan. Bengal, in eastern India, became a major indigo producer. Historians know the Greeks

A piece of indigo plant dye from India

The color indigo

and Romans considered it a luxury, and that a thousand years later Marco Polo saw it during his travels. But indigo's real heyday came after the Renaissance, when Europeans planted it in warm weather colonies and imported slaves to work the fields.

Bengal and what became Bangladesh also produced jute, a hardy plant fiber. Colored gold, fairly easy to grow, thriving on the warm and rainy monsoon, jute was an essential product in the region for centuries, as a source of clothing as well as everyday items like rope.

India was also the source of a now-popular animal fiber. Kashmiris harvested a type of fine wool from cashmere goats and related species native to the soaring Himalayas. Called pashmina by the Persians and cashmere in modern times, the wool was crafted by hand into shawls mentioned in Afghan accounts as early as the third century BCE. Cashmere was (and is) well known for its combination of strength, lightness, and softness.

The Indus Valley Civilization may have made one other contribution to fashion. Some historians have theorized that buttons made of seashell, and used as decorations rather than for closing clothes, originated in the IVC before 2600 BCE.

King of Gems

Sanskrit speakers called the diamond *vajra*, "thunderbolt."
In ancient times, much like today, it was considered the
king of gemstones. Mined in south-central India, the
diamond was already considered valuable in 300 BCE.
At approximately that time a government official in the
Maurya dynasty described the stone's uses and virtues in
a document. Other writings, two centuries older, mention
vajra, as well. India's diamond industry may go back
thousands of years.

In ancient times, miners could find diamonds in the silt
of streambeds. Water carried the stones from deposits thrust
upward by geological processes from areas deep within the
earth. Diamonds later came from mines. Until 1725, India
was the world's only major source of diamonds.

Indians attributed great powers to the stone. According
to a Buddhist study of gems called the *Ratnapariksa*:

> He who, having pure body, always carries a
> diamond with sharp points, without blemish,
> free from all faults; that one, as long as he
> lives, knows each day will bear some things:
> happiness, prosperity, children, riches, grain,
> cows and meat. He who wears [such] a
> diamond will see dangers recede from him
> whether he be threatened by serpents, fire,
> poison, sickness, thieves, flood or evil spirits.

The *Ratnapariksa* also noted that every diamond
belonged to one of four color groups. Each of the four
castes was associated with a certain color. Only the
Brahmin ruling caste might own the most valuable white
diamonds, and they could also own those belonging to the
three lower castes.

As the text made clear, Indians developed a complex system of grading diamond quality and assigned different attributes to spots, misplaced points and edges, and other imperfections. The *Ratnapariksa*'s writers also recognized diamond was harder than any other stone or metal.

Though famed as a gemstone, diamond had practical uses. Indian and Chinese craftsmen used the stone to drill holes in beads. Diamond worked Chinese jade, and it is possible it carved designs in Roman jewelry. But any other uses, if there were any, remain unknown.

Trade by land and sea eventually delivered diamonds—probably very few of them—to Rome. The soldier-scholar Pliny said the gem possessed the greatest value of all human possessions and repeated an Indian belief that a diamond was an antidote to poison. Indians, however, seem to have kept most diamonds for themselves during the Roman era. That would change starting in the 900s.

Invaders

The first wave of Islamic invasions had stopped in far western India in the eighth century. A second, and more significant, wave arrived 250 years later.

In 997, the Muslim prince Mahmud succeeded his late father. Needing to provide work and rewards for his large army, and eager to conquer non-believers, Mahmud began to raid, then invade, northwestern India. For thirty-plus years he looted cities, destroyed Hindu temples, killed untold numbers of Indians, and carried off treasure of every kind.

Mahmud's Ghaznavid Empire was just one early Muslim state within India. Other invaders followed, all eager for power and treasure, and to assert Islamic supremacy. Their victories gave Muslim merchants access to diamonds. Increased traffic in the stones delivered diamonds to outlets in the vast Muslim trade networks. The diamond trade soon took root in Venice, Europe's rising merchant superpower.

The kingdom of Golkonda, in south central India, first rose in the 1360s. The Hindu Kakatiyas ruled Golkonda initially and built a fort in their capital, also called Golkonda. The kingdom soon became part of two major Islamic empires, however. Each added to the fort until it was a complex of four forts. By the 1500s, Muslim merchants kept Golkonda diamonds in the forts en route to the city's booming market in gems. The famous Hope Diamond, now at the Smithsonian Natural History Museum, and the Koh-i-Noor ("Mountain of Light") in the British crown jewels, supposedly came from stones taken out of Golkonda's mines.

Evalyn Walsh McLean, wife of *Washington Post* scion Edward McLean, wearing the Hope Diamond, sometime between 1905 and 1945. The McLeans owned the diamond for many years.

Miraculous Wootz

Indian metalworkers manufactured a special type of steel that was one of the hardest man-made substances in the ancient world. Called *ukku* in southern India, and usually referred to as wootz in today's English, the material may have been created as early as 500 BCE. Archaeologists have found only limited physical evidence for that date. But written texts of the era refer to it, and tradition and many modern historians usually date it to that time, if not earlier.

Making wootz built on earlier advances in iron making, a technology known to the Harappans and Arya. To create wootz, a manufacturer first heated porous iron. Workers used hammers to beat a waste product called slag from the hot iron. Ancient furnaces could not quite heat up enough to melt iron, but the process weakened it enough to allow workers to knock it into pieces. It next went into a clay crucible, or container, with wood chips and other plant material. Heating the crucible with hot charcoal raised the temperatures inside. Burning wood released carbon, and as the melting iron absorbed the carbon it became steel, a much stronger metal. Workers then allowed the steel to cool and harden into easily transported bars or cakes.

Contact with the Muslim world led to the creation of the most famous wootz product: weapons made of so-called Damascus steel.

A blade forged from Damascus steel was harder and held its edge longer—great advantages in combat. Arab manufacturers imported wootz from India in bar form and turned it into swords, knives, and armor. The city of Damascus became a center of wootz smithing, and gave the extraordinary alloy the name used across the Middle East and Europe. Indian smiths also manufactured weapons.

Indian steel makers kept their process a secret. Muslims, in turn, obscured where wootz came from, as they did with other valuable Indian products.

Damascus steel blades and armor sit in museums around the world. But no one knows how to make them anymore. High quality weapons rolled out of workshops until about 1750. Inferior imitations were made into the next century. Then the secret of Damascus steel arms vanished into history. Current-day metallurgists, despite hard work and research, have yet to recreate the technology behind the legendary swords.

The Forever Pillar

Rulers intend for the monuments they build to last for a long time, if not forever. Chandragupta II, patron of the master poet Kalidasa and ruler of the Gupta dynasty from about 380–413, succeeded where many others failed.

Sometime during his reign—we're not sure when—Chandragupta II ordered the raising of an iron pillar amidst a collection of Jain temples at a place known as Vishnupadagiri, located roughly thirty-one miles (fifty kilometers) east of modern-day Bhopal, India.

Chandragupta II dedicated the pillar to Vishnu, the supreme god in many Hindu traditions. Standing twenty-three feet, eight inches (7.21 meters) high, albeit with three feet, eight inches (1.12 m) below ground, the Iron Pillar weighed approximately six tons. When placed at Vishnupadagiri, it served as an astronomical tool measuring the seasons, as well as a monument. And like many monuments, the Iron Pillar carried a message into the future. The words celebrate the military victories by Chandra (a shortened version of Chandragupta) and praise Vishnu.

The Pillar is 98 percent iron. Rust, or hydrated iron oxide, is a common enemy of iron. To the amazement of metallurgists, the Pillar today shows almost no signs of rusting, despite 1600 years of being exposed to the elements. (Slight rusting may be taking place below ground.)

It appears that phosphorus and certain particles in the iron, along with the purity of the metal, combine to form a protective layer of film that protects the Pillar. Rust forms

Iron Pillar erected by Chandragupta II, within
Qutb complex, in Merauli, Delhi

on the film but doesn't eat into the Pillar itself. Some researchers claim that different factors, such as the mild climate and the longtime ritual of smearing butter on the Pillar, have played a role.

The Iron Pillar now stands in Delhi as part of the ruins surrounding the Qutb Minar, a red sandstone minaret built to compliment the Quwwatu-il-Islam, Delhi's first mosque. Qutbu'd-Din Aibak, the first Islamic ruler of Delhi, began the construction of the Qutb Minar in 1202. Some traditions have it that earlier rulers brought the Iron Pillar to Delhi in the eleventh century. Another states Iltutmish, Qutbu'd-Din Aibak's former slave and trusted official, brought the Pillar to the city after he took power in the early 1200s.

Useful Materials

India developed other essential early technologies shared by other cultures. Ceramic making, discovered independently in the Western Hemisphere as well as in the Old World, was known to the Harappans and their neighbors.

Evidence of glassmaking also dates to India's ancient era. Glass beads used in ornaments, jewelry, and even as currency played a role in several early civilizations, India's included. A small-scale bead industry in north and northwest India goes back before 1000 BCE and probably started much earlier. Peoples in far southern India also made glass. In 2009, archaeologists announced the discovery of thousands of beads and a furnace for glassmaking in the Tamil Nadu state. It dated to the early years of the Common Era.

People in India mined zinc at Zawar, in northwest India. Historians speculate Zawar zinc went into the creation of brass, an alloy of zinc and copper. Zawar began providing large amounts of zinc in the 1200s. The next century, Indian alchemists were creating medical balms, ointments, and other treatments made of zinc mixed with butter, mustard, and dried cherry-plums.

Today zinc is the fourth-most-used metal in the world, and India is a major producer. The Zawar mines remain in operation.

Game of the Mind

Though not exactly a technology, the game of chess developed into a tool for training in fields as diverse as mathematics and military tactics. Chess's most direct known ancestor, *chaturanga*, enters history in the 500s. *Chaturanga* probably grew out of older pastimes from lands in contact with India as well as within India itself. It shared some traits with modern chess, such as the presence of a king and pawns. But *chaturanga* was not played on a checkerboard, it involved four players, and the pieces often moved in different ways and included a counselor and an elephant.

Most popular games included dice or something else that added a random element to play. Chaturanga did not. Luck had no place with this new game. A player competed against another player, not chance; intellect and intellect only ruled the board.

By coincidence, or maybe not, chess emerged at the same time Indians had unlocked advanced mathematical concepts like the idea of zero and the use of decimals and negative numbers. Analyzing chess strategy using math became common among those in search of strategic secrets and a deeper understanding of the game.

Muslims encountered the Indian game when they conquered Persia. They transformed *chaturanga* into *shatranj*, a new game played on a black-and-white board and much closer to chess. *Shatranj* became a phenomenon throughout the Islamic world. Though played for enjoyment, the game was also exalted as a bloodless war game that trained the mind for strategy and deep contemplation while fulfilling Muhammad's command to acquire knowledge. It was from Muslim lands that *shatranj* and similar games spread to Europe—where play boomed in medieval times—and became what we know as chess.

Rani Ki vav is a famous stepwell situated in Gujarat in India. Built during the last decade of the eleventh century by Rani Udaymati in memory of her husband, Bhimdeva I of the Chalukya Dynasty, the vav is decorated with around eight hundred stone sculptures and reliefs. There are impressive images of Gods of the Hindu pantheon in their various incarnations with their consorts.

Stepwells

Between 200 and 400, an architectural innovation, the stepwell, took root in Gujarat. Called a vav in Gujarati, virtually invisible on the surface, the stepwells were multi-level water storage structures cut downward into rock. Straight staircases led down into a well shaft. Each level had a landing and rows of columns for support and decoration. The stepwell allowed visitors to gather water while socializing rather than the usual arduous chore of drawing up water one container at a time.

In the eleventh century, the plain stepwells of the early era suddenly evolved into spectacular underground temples. The carved walls featured religious sculpture and ornate decoration.

In 1060, local rulers sponsored the creation of the stunning Rani Ki (Queen's Well) vav at Patan. Watched over by reliefs of the god Vishnu's avatars (personifications) and attendants, Rani Ki vav was more than a water source. Women—usually tasked with getting water—could pray and conduct religious rituals away from the strict rules of traditional Hindu temples, as well as bathe and visit with neighbors in a comfortably cool setting. Those things had real social and personal value, as Hindu culture often treated women as second-class citizens. Noblewomen paid for the construction of some vavs.

Conquering Muslims adopted the stepwell idea. An Islamic vav kept the columns. But since Islam forbade sculpture and other images, Muslim builders decorated their vavs with inscriptions and geometric and floral patterns.

Vav building spread to the Rajasthan area. Archaeologists estimate a thousand vavs of various sizes may exist.

Most, however, no longer function as they did of old. In the 1800s, the British authorities in charge in Gujarat closed the vavs over health concerns. The boom in water use in modern Gujarat has lowered the underground water table so far that the wells inside the vavs have gone dry. Many are filled with silt, though that offers an upside. Silt helped preserve Rani Ki's interior for centuries.

Indian archaeologists began excavating it in the 1950s. Authorities in Gujarat hope to land it on the list of UNESCO World Heritage Sites.

Chapter Four:
Indian Medicine

Peoples around the world have practiced medicine since prehistoric times. Systems of medicine developed as societies became more complex. India's ancient system, like China's, continues to be the medical care of choice for millions of people in the twenty-first century.

As medical historian Roy Porter pointed out, Indian medicine owes its longevity to a strong resistance to change. The reasons for that resistance go back to the ancient idea that divine sources passed down medical knowledge to humanity in the distant past. Since medicine had appeared in a perfect (divine) form, there was no need to make changes. The belief led generations of practitioners to defend old traditions against corrupt outside influences rather than seek out new solutions to medical problems. It also gave the ancient ideas extraordinary staying power and influence.

A Long and Healthy Life

Traditional Indian medicine is called *Ayurveda*, from the Sanskrit words for long life (*ayus*) and knowledge (*veda*).

In simplest terms, the Ayurvedic philosophy preached moderation. Food, exercise, sex, sleep, and medical treatment—while important—should never be overdone. Prevention of problems was a priority. Physicians offered detailed advice on everyday aspects of care like bathing, washing out the eyes, drinking the proper amount of water with a meal, and using twigs—from specific kinds of trees—to clean the teeth. Hindu religious belief influenced some ideas within Ayurveda, such as an imbalance in one's soul as a cause of disease, and the relationship of good health to being in harmony with the universe.

The Vedas mention medical matters, including the prevalence of disease, but provide few details. Historians associate Ayurveda with a later era. According to tradition it drew on the Vedas and other older teachings. But how it did, even if it did, is still being argued by historians. Whatever the case, Ayurveda was very different from the medicine of the Vedas.

Two texts, both massive, form the core of Ayurveda. According to tradition, a sage named Caraka authored *Caraka Samhita*, or Caraka's Compendium. Sushruta, another sage, supposedly wrote the second text, the *Sushruta Samhita*, at the ancient holy city of Benares (now Varanasi). The dates of both remain uncertain. In fact, it's not clear that the individuals Caraka or Sushruta really existed or, if they did, when they lived. Though many sources claim the Samhitas appeared in very ancient times, historians usually date Caraka's work to the early years of the Common Era, and Sushruta's to sometime between the last years BCE to the 300s. Parts, however, may go back to 400 BCE. It is also accepted that some of what the two sages describe had been part of Indian medical practice for centuries.

Together the texts cover a vast number of topics including anatomy, techniques for examining and diagnosing patients, treatments, surgery, medicinal plants, the creation and application of medicines, and details on hundreds of diseases from asthma to plague, and hundreds of conditions, from pregnancy to insanity.

Other important Ayurvedic texts appeared in later centuries. The writer Madhavakara, writing around the year 700, sorted medical problems by category or theme, a revision adopted in many future works.

From Virtue to Vaidya

Medicine may have once drawn from the Brahmin (priests), Kshatriya (warriors), and Vaishya (merchant) castes, but the Brahmins dominated the profession as the Common Era went on. Students studying Ayurveda learned their occupation while living by a strict code. They vowed to live celibate, vegetarian, sober, nonviolent lives, and to follow the commands of their guru (teacher).

They also learned lifelong rules to never abandon a patient, to keep a patient's medical matters private, and to only treat a woman in the presence of her husband or another male relative. Modest dress was a must, as was total honesty. "Everyone admires a . . . physician who is courteous, wise, self-disciplined, and a master of his subject," Caraka said.

While Ayurvedic texts were important, students learned on the job, with the guru passing down a wealth of information in oral and practical form. At the end of the training period (perhaps seven years), the student took a test. Graduates became a *vaidya*, one who knows—an Ayurveda, a physician.

But training did not end at graduation. The physician was expected to improve his skills and acquire new knowledge for as long as he practiced. To do so he not only attended physicians' conferences to exchange information, he learned folk medicine from farmers, tribal rain forest peoples, and others with obscure knowledge.

Medieval miniature out of the Toggenburg Bible (Switzerland) of 1411.
The disease in this miniature is generally interpreted as a depiction of
the plague, or the Black Death, though, the location of bumps or blisters
is more consistent with smallpox (as the bubonic plague normally
causes them only in the groin and in the armpits).

A physician studied internal medicine, surgery and anatomy, ear-nose-throat, pediatrics (children's medicine), psychiatry (in part related to possession by demons), poisons, fertility, and prolonging life. Beginning as students, physicians also learned how to mix medicines. This pharmacology training covered a lot of ground, with cooking, the study of metal and creation of metal compounds, and making sugar among the necessary skills. Growing medicinal plants was also an important subject, as Ayurveda relied overwhelmingly on plant-based medicines.

In Balance

Ayurveda sought good health through the balance of air, bile, and phlegm, the three so-called humors or *dosas*. Each *dosa* represented a force of the natural world: air (wind), fire (the sun), or water (the moon). Each *dosa* covered a set of biological functions. For example, *pitta* (fire, the sun) represented health in digestion, body heat, blood, the brain, sight, and the complexion. The body consisted of seven tissue types that included bone, flesh, and blood. The 107 *marmas* marked important organs, nerves, veins and arteries, and muscles.

Sushruta identified 1,120 diseases. Not all arose from imbalances in the dosa, he said. Invisible organisms in the blood caused disease. Sushruta's insight into the power of viruses and bacteria to upset human health predates scientific proof of either by more than a thousand years.

Thanks to the *Sushruta Samhita*, modern historians know tuberculosis, leprosy, various fevers (some probably malaria), and smallpox existed in ancient India. One breakthrough concerned smallpox.

A deadly virus that covered victims in pustules and often left survivors scarred, smallpox had afflicted people in Eurasia and Africa since prehistory. By 1000 CE, inoculation against smallpox appears to have entered Indian medicine, though it is not mentioned in the Samhitas, or in any other Sanskrit text. Possibly the idea for inoculation came from

the field of Ayurveda devoted to poisons. Both Charaka
and Sushruta noted that certain toxic substances—if
used the right way—made effective medicines. The idea
behind smallpox inoculation, that is, purposely infecting
a person with a mild case of smallpox to prevent a
serious case later on, is similar.

Surgery

The *Sushruta Samhita* was regarded as a guide and
reference work for the science of surgery (called *Alya*,
Sanskrit for arrow). Sushruta explained various kinds of
bandages and listed 121 instruments—ideally made of
steel—used in surgical procedures. The text also offered
advice on surgical training. Since Hindu belief forbade
working on or even touching a corpse, would-be surgeons
had to be creative with the materials at hand.

> The art of making specific forms of incision
> should be taught by making cuts in the
> body of a [gourd], bottle gourd, watermelon,
> cucumber. . . . The art of making excisions
> should be practically demonstrated by making
> openings in the body of a full water bag or in
> the bladder of a dead animal, or in the side of
> a leather pouch full of slime or water. The art
> of scraping should be instructed on a piece
> of skin on which the hair has been allowed
> to remain. . . . The art of probing and stuffing
> should be taught on worm-eaten wood, or
> on the reed of a bamboo, or on the mouth
> of a dried [bottle gourd]. . . . [T]he art of
> bandaging . . . should be practically learned
> by tying bandages round the specific limbs
> and members of a full-sized doll made of
> stuffed linen.

An illustration of the famed Hindi surgeon Sushruta, as he is about to form an artificial earlobe for a patient. Known as the father of surgery, Sushruta is the author of *Sushruta Samhita*, in which he describes more than 120 surgical instruments, three hundred surgical procedures, and classifies human surgery into eight categories.

As for actual surgery, Sushruta carried on with the Ayurvedic penchant for categorization by sorting operations into eight categories: incision, excision (amputation), scarring, aspiration, extraction, probing, draining, and stitching.

Indian physicians performed surgery on all parts of the body. Surgeons opened the abdomen to address hernias and other problems, and to deliver babies via caesarian section. Limbs were removed, tonsils drawn out, polyps taken from the larynx, battle wounds sewn closed.

Sushruta described the earliest known practice of plastic surgery. Ayurvedic plastic surgery covered folding over skin to cover minor defects or wounds. Sushruta focused in particular on the ear and nose. He described fifteen ways to use skin from a patient's cheek to rebuild a torn earlobe. It was a common injury in parts of India. A baby traditionally had its ears pierced at a young age. Heavy ornaments hung from the ears, however, often mangled or detached the lobe, necessitating surgery.

Nose reconstruction also had cultural significance. Religious and political authorities in India—paralleling many other cultures—sometimes sentenced people convicted of adultery (especially women), theft, or other crimes to have their nose cut off. Using tissue from the cheek or sometimes the forehead, the surgeon crafted a new nose over the stump of the old and inserted small pipes for nostrils. Several rounds of bandages, plus treatment with powders and oils, helped with healing.

Finally, Sushruta suggested using wine, sometimes mixed with other ingredients, as anesthesia and to kill post-surgical pain. An obscure herbal drug, *sammohini*, was also used to knock out patients for surgery.

Possible Buddhist Contributions

Buddhism seems to have rejected the knowledge in the Vedas when it came to medicine, as it did on many other topics. On medical matters the Buddhist texts have far more in common with Ayurveda, and Buddhist medical practice may have influenced it.

Buddhists believed in medicine. Monks seeking to escape desire of earthly things carried very little in the way of possessions. But they were allowed basic traditional remedies like oil, honey, and butter. Later Buddhist writings offered information on treatments and how to use herbs as medicine. Monks thereafter drew from a more diverse Ayurvedic medicine cabinet.

In the 300s, some Buddhist temples seem to have included sick rooms. The tradition may go back much further. Possible forerunners of hospitals, these sick rooms may have first given care to monks before expanding to aid local communities. Ashoka, as part of his patronage of Buddhism, was said to have included hospital construction in his public works program.

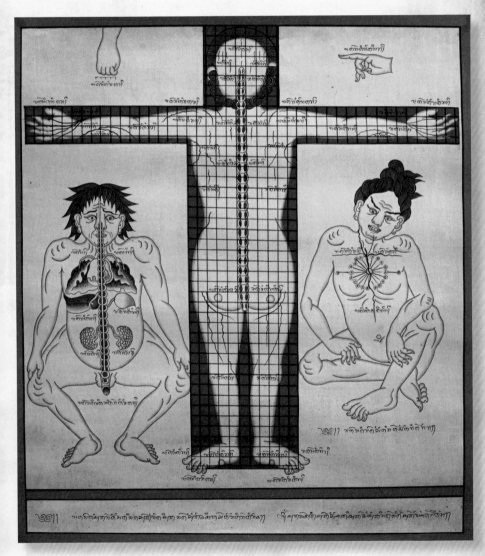

A Buddhist medical *Thangka* from Nepal. A *Thangka* is a painting on silk with embroidery.

Ibn Sina

The Muslim invasions after 1000 BCE brought Islamic medicine to India. Referred to as *Yunani*, a word Indians used to mean foreigners, the new medical lore was actually a reinterpretation of ancient Greek and Roman medicine. Ibn Sina, an Islamic scholar born around 980, organized all the known medicine into a multivolume encyclopedia called *The Canon of Medicine*. Considered a masterpiece of medieval science, the *Canon* revived much forgotten ancient knowledge. In the medieval and Renaissance eras it served as a bible of medicine in Europe as well as the Islamic world. Translations of the work reached as far as China.

As well as discussing all known aspects of medical science, Ibn Sina laid out how to test a medicine's effectiveness according to scientific measurement and observation. Evidence, not faith or tradition, guided his system. His methods share common ground with modern-day techniques like clinical trials and animal testing. One entire volume of his *Canon* listed more than seven hundred medications, with Ibn Sina's discussion of each. Yunani medicine and Ayurveda soon borrowed from one another.

The *Canon*'s other contributions to science include Ibn Sina's description of skin diseases, his awareness of the dangers of high blood pressure, his belief that many diseases spread via water or dirt, notes on the structure of the eye, and suggestions for cancer treatment.

The Yunani system, like Ayurveda, remains in use today. Many Muslims, especially those living outside of cities, trust it as traditional Islamic medicine, and visit physicians called hakims.

Chapter Five:
Spices of Life

About 1224 BCE (or maybe closer to 1213 BCE), Ramses II, one of the most accomplished pharaohs of Ancient Egypt, died after a sixty-plus year reign. As the reverent Egyptians prepared Ramses's body for mummification, they inserted peppercorns into his nostrils. Peppercorns are dried berries from a climbing vine botanists now call *Piper nigrum*, or black pepper. *Piper nigrum* did not grow in Egypt. It did not grow anywhere near Egypt. Black pepper came from India.

India traded with the outside world centuries before Ramses. Archaeologists studying the ancient Mesopotamian civilization have found seashells native to southern India's waters with other relics dating to before 2000 BCE. The implication is that the Mesopotamians acquired the shells in trade. Whether they dealt directly with Indians, or with other peoples who had traded for India's goods, can probably never be known.

First- or second- (or third-) hand contact continued. Sumerian records found in the same general region mention trade with a place called Meluhhaa, a source of rare products. Meluhhaa may have referred to the Indus Valley Civilization. Archaeologists have also found Indus Valley seals in Sumerian lands. Experts believe the IVC's wealth relied on a complex economic system based in part on such far-ranging trade networks.

Many materials used by Indus Valley craftsmen must have come from somewhere else through trade, since such materials aren't found in IVC lands or nearby areas. Trade with faraway lands probably took place by sea, with Indian ships carrying products to Sumeria and the Arabian Peninsula. Goods returned to Indus Valley cities by the same routes.

Trade also took place—and created wealth—within the Indus Valley network of cities and towns. Merchants and customers in Harappa and elsewhere were aided by the use of the standard weights and measures used throughout the empire. Standardization allowed goods to be weighed, counted, and priced the same way everywhere, a far smoother operation than forcing traders to learn a new measurement and monetary systems for each town.

Land of Spice

Ancient India's most important trade, however, originated on the southwest coast of the Indian peninsula. The Malabar Coast was a narrow strip of land between the Indian Ocean and mountains called the Western Ghats. The monsoon rains trapped by the mountains soak the jungles and nearby plain from around the first of June until November. The winds then shift and blow dry air from Asia's mainland.

It is during the dry season that farmers harvested Malabar's spices. In general, a spice is defined as a strong

tasting and/or strong smelling product made from any part of a plant other than its leaves. (Leaves typically are called herbs.) Ancient peoples used a variety of spices in food and as sacrifices, and perhaps most importantly in medicines. Demand made Malabar Coast spices among the most valuable products in the ancient world—and for long centuries after.

A handful of spices fueled the region's financial success: cardamom, its relative ginger, cinnamon and the less desirable "false" cinnamon called cassia, and the most valuable spice of all, black pepper.

Raw black pepper

Cardamom

Strong tasting, even today one of the most expensive spices on the market, cardamom comes from a stalky, large-leaf plant that grew across South Asia. Indian and Sri Lankan cardamom was considered a "true" cardamom, as opposed to the less valuable "false" types that grew elsewhere. Farmers extracted the spice by picking the plant's triangular fruit before it ripened. As the fruit dried it turned green and hardened. Cardamom seeds, the source of its odor and flavor, formed inside a pod. Transporting the spice in its pod form allowed it to retain its potency through long journeys.

Indians used cardamom to flavor a wide variety of foods. Arabians imported it to put in their coffee, a tradition that continues today. Its odor made it a desirable perfume ingredient and people chewed it to freshen the breath. Premodern medicine, meanwhile, prescribed cardamom as a treatment for sore throats and bronchitis. Adding it to tea supposedly calmed the stomach. Some people used it as a stimulant or to treat fevers.

Cardamom pods

Ginger root

Ginger

Zingiber officinale evolved in southern China before spreading to India and other parts of Asia. The spice ginger comes from its dried rhizome (an underground stem). Another spice with long use in Indian cuisine, ginger came in a wide variety of flavors, from bold to subtle, and from hot to mild. The strength of its flavor and odor depended on factors such as growing conditions and breeding.

Ginger was (and is) a mainstay of Chinese medicine. It has an ancient history as a treatment for stomach gas and other digestive problems. Americans have drunk ginger ale, made with ginger oil, for a stomachache or nausea for more than a hundred years. Ginger in soup or tea traditionally treated colds and other respiratory discomforts, and it was said to provide energy to those in need of a boost.

Cinnamon and Cassia

Cinnamon originated on Sri Lanka, the droplet-shaped island off India's southern coast. People there probably used it as early as prehistoric times. It spread to, and became a product of, the Malabar Coast. True cinnamon came from the dried bark of the cinnamon tree *Cinnamomum verum*. A few of its cousins, most famously *C. cassia*, produced cassia, a more common and less desirable spice often called false cinnamon or Chinese cinnamon.

Harvesters gathered cinnamon by loosening the cinnamon-laden inner bark from the outer bark. The inner bark came off in curled strips. Once cleaned, a number of strips were rolled into long, thin quills, what the Venetians of the thirteenth century would call *canella* (little cannon tubes). A buyer bought this many quills or that much of a single quill.

Cinnamon sticks

Egyptians used cinnamon to embalm the dead. The Old Testament mentions cinnamon as an ingredient in the Hebrews' holy oil and incense, and suggests it was also used as an air freshener. Some cultures sacrificed the valuable spice to their gods. Arabians cooked with cinnamon. Medical uses included the treatment of stomach problems and snakebites, as a way of getting rid of freckles, and it found use as a stimulant. It also made bad tasting medicines easier to swallow, no small matter in eras when physicians used ingredients like clay, dung, and animal parts in their prescriptions.

Cassia may have reached Greece as early as the seventh century BCE. The ancient Greeks knew it differed from cinnamon. The two spices were hard to tell apart. Less than honest spice merchants seem to have mixed cassia with cinnamon to stretch their supply of the more valuable spice. Cassia's taste was stronger and its texture rougher than true cinnamon. Like cinnamon, cassia found its way into the Hebrew oil and incense, and Chinese physicians used it in treatments.

Pepper

Today many Americans see pepper as a common condiment on kitchen counters and restaurant tables. Its humble modern role masks pepper's importance in world history. Peoples in ancient times on through to the Renaissance considered black pepper one of the world's most desirable, and costliest, substances, and went to great lengths to find it and control it.

Both black pepper and the weaker flavored white pepper came from *Piper nigrum*. Many varieties of *Piper nigrum* grow in Kerala, a large southwestern region that includes part of the Malabar Coast. A plant tends to evolve into varied forms in its place of origin, since it has been there so long. For that reason botanists believe the pepper vine originated in the low altitude forests of the Ghats.

A mixture of black, green, and pink peppercorns

Indian growers picked the peppercorns before they ripened. The fruit blackened as it dried. It could be shipped as dried peppercorns or after it was ground into a powder. Making white pepper involved picking somewhat more ripe berries and was prepared somewhat differently.

Indians cooked with pepper thousands of years ago. Pepper spiced food in the *Mahabharata* and turned up as a medicine in Sanskrit medical texts. Buddhist monks, forbidden most possessions, could carry pepper as a medicine. Ancient physicians in various parts of the world used it to treat ailments from stomach problems to gangrene to toothaches, and many more besides.

The cultivation of these spices has spread around the world in the last five hundred years. But prior to that, the spice trade made India a major player in commercial networks that stretched over land and sea from Great Britain and Portugal in the west to Indonesia and Japan in the east.

Arabian Marketplace

Trade in Indian pepper probably existed 4,000 years ago. Caravans on land carried Indian products along the Indus River to the mountains of the Hindu Kush. Once the traders crossed the mountains, they followed a series of routes, called by historians the Silk Roads, linking China to lands further west.

The ancient sea trade in spices went through the Arabian Peninsula. Though it is easy shorthand to refer to the merchants as Arabs, there were distinct Arabian civilizations. Each profited from the spice trade.

Arab and probably transplanted Indian merchants in coastal Arabian seaports brought in India's pepper, marked up the price, and shipped it on via the Red Sea to the Middle East. Other merchants in the chain added their markup. The seafaring Phoenicians, based in the Mediterranean, received the goods overland, marked up the price yet again, and took the trade from there further west. Distance and the hazards of long-distance travel, plus the many markups, kept the price of pepper sky high. Pharaohs and kings were among the few able to afford it.

A very few ancient Greek writings contain vague mentions of pepper in recipes and medicines. It probably remained a product for the rich. In 332 BCE, Alexander the Great of Macedon, a Greek state, destroyed Tyre, a major Phoenician trading city. His new Egyptian metropolis, Alexandria, replaced Tyre as the center of Mediterranean trade.

Alexander's far-flung military campaigns eventually led him all the way to western India. It's possible the related activity disrupted the overland pepper trade. He might have affected the sea trade, too, had fate not intervened. But Alexander's death in 323 BCE stopped his planned attack on Arabia. Greeks based in Alexandria, meanwhile, took over the Mediterranean pepper trade.

The savvy Arabs, hoping to discourage competitors, obscured the origins of spices with tall tales. For generations Europeans heard stories of gigantic birds that built nests of cinnamon sticks. Herodotus, writing in Greece in the fifth century BCE, reported:

> [The Arabs] cut all the oxen and asses and beasts of burden that die . . . into large pieces . . . and the old birds, swooping down, seize the pieces of meat and fly away with them up to their nests; which, not being able to support the weight, break off and fall to the ground. Hereupon the Arabians return and collect the cinnamon.

Gathering cassia was said to be even more hazardous. A worker had to cover his entire body in animal hides and battle batlike creatures to collect the spice from lakes. That the spices actually came from plants in India was a carefully guarded secret.

Monsoons and Merchants

The geographer Strabo wrote that the Sabeans, a spice-trading Arabian people, had become so rich they decorated their houses with ivory, gold, and precious stones. By the time Strabo told his tale, however, the Romans were in the process of ending Arabia's control of the spice trade.

The change began in 30 BCE, when Roman forces defeated the Egyptian queen Cleopatra. Egypt became a province of the Roman Empire, and Egypt's ports on the Red Sea opened up to Roman ships. Suddenly Rome's spice merchants had the means to bypass the Arabian ports and sail to the Malabar Coast to make their own deals. According to Strabo, an armada of 120 Roman trading ships left for India each year. Gigantic freighters, some of the largest sea vessels of ancient times, made up the heart of the fleet.

Contact with India put to rest the old myths about giant birds and other creatures. Pliny, in his works on natural history, discussed the science and uses of spice plants. His contemporary Dioscorides, a physician, wrote on the medicinal uses of spices.

Initially it took a Roman fleet two years to make the round trip to and from India. Pirates and storms menaced the ships, but the prices to be had for Malabar pepper and other Indian products made the journey worth the risks. Then, in the first century CE, an unknown mariner wrote the *Periplus of the Erythraean Sea,* a guide for those sailing the waters between the Red Sea and India. The *Periplus* contained a wealth of information on ports along the route and the merchandise dealt in each one.

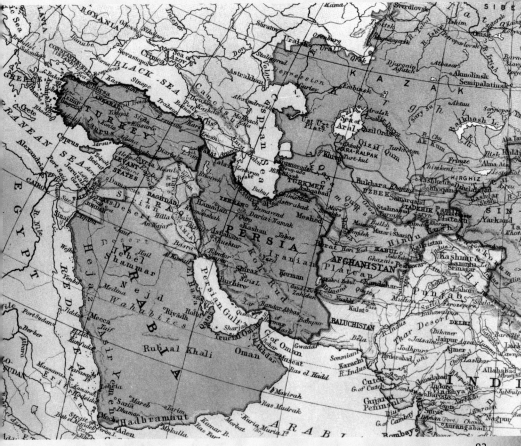

A map of the Middle East from a photographer's logbook, dated 1934-1939

As importantly, however, it also revealed the secret that had allowed the Arabs to control the spice trade.

The *Periplus*'s author mentioned the observations of Hippalus, an Alexandrian Greek sailor who had worked the spice run to India. Hippalus had described the monsoon winds, the seasonal cycle of air movements that governed weather, and sailing, in the Indian Ocean. Understanding the monsoon unlocked Indian Ocean travel for the Romans. The empire's ships could now run to India and back in a single year—half as long as before. The sea trade soon eclipsed the land trade.

An India fleet left Egypt and headed down the Red Sea to stops in either southern Arabia or at the Cape of Spices, on the horn of Africa that poked into the Indian Ocean. Ships involved in the Africa trade turned south to buy ivory, wild animals, and other goods. Spice ships bound for India caught the stormy southwest monsoon in their sails for the eastward journey. If all went well, the fleet crossed to the Malabar Coast in under six weeks and dropped their anchors in September.

The *Periplus* stated that ships could visit up to nineteen bustling ports, each on a river, to deal wine, wheat, gold and silver coins, coral, and glass and copper items manufactured in Roman factories.

These goods purchased Malabar pepper, first and foremost, but the Romans bought cassia as well as other spices. For example, Indian traders bundled *tejpat* leaves for sale. Romans called the plant *malabathron*. It was another relative of cinnamon, one that provided an oil used in makeup and perfumes. Costus, a root from Kashmir, had similar uses. In addition, Roman merchants purchased sapphires, rubies, and the other gems mined in India; rare animals like tigers and peacocks; teak, an exotic wood; and silk the Indian traders had imported from China. All that and more came via shipping, over the Western Ghats on animals, wagons, or human backs, or down whichever river flowed into the city.

A Bengal tiger wading in water

Dry monsoon winds from the northeast blew the fully loaded Roman fleets toward home. The Romans added a number of new ports to the Red Sea to accommodate the booming India trade. Cargo unloaded from ships went onto camel caravans that hauled the goods overland to the Nile River. Barges brought the products to Alexandria. Freighters carried pepper and the rest to Ostia, the port downriver from Rome. There, India's emeralds and elephants, its ivory and onyx, ended a journey counted in the thousands of miles.

On Shore, at Sea

India's trade went beyond sending rarities to Rome. First and foremost, Indians traded with other Indians. The growth of India's cities—with greater concentrations of both producers and customers—was a major factor in fueling an ever-more complex economy. India's craftsmen, traders, and other professionals organized into guilds around their specialties. Each member agreed to follow a code of conduct in return for protection, loans, and access to markets, among other advantages.

On land, the ancient city of Taxila, in the western Punjab, served as a gateway to the west. Caravans passed through Taxila on the royal road that connected the city with distant Petaliputra, an important Ganges River city that had been Ashoka's capital at the height of the Maurya Empire. Beyond Taxila ran the Silk Roads and other routes that connected India to the Middle East and, eventually, the Mediterranean, and also to China.

Taxila, an important archaelogical site in Pakistan. From the fifth century BCE to the second century CE, it was an important Buddhist center of learning. Also, Taxila illustrates the different stages in the development of a city on the Indus that was alternately influenced by Persia, Greece, and Central Asia.

Indian ships moved east as well as west, however. Merchants bound for Southeast Asia departed from eastern seaboard ports and either followed the coast to places like Cambodia or Java, or used the Malacca Strait en route to China. Indian traders created overseas communities in Burma, Malaya, Bali, and other stops along the sea lanes.

The eastern trade was extensive and lucrative. Around 1280, Chinese officials in Hangzhou told the Venetian traveler Marco Polo that 10,000 pounds of pepper came into the city every day.

Outsiders also set up enclaves in India's cities. Indians referred to the foreigners from regions west of India as *Yavana* or *Unani* or *Yona*. (The Yunani medicine brought by Muslims was another alternative spelling.) Indians used Yavana in reference to many different peoples, including Greeks, the Bactrians of Central Asia, and Arabians. Considered *mleccha* (a word that could mean alien, low, or barbaric, among other things), Yavana fell outside the Hindu caste system and were therefore considered "undesirable." Changes in religious practice would one day make trading with Yavana a problem for Hindu merchants.

Changing Tastes

As Rome imported more pepper, the increase in supply lowered its price, making it available to more people throughout the Empire. Archaeologists have found evidence of pepper use across the Roman world, from kitchens to garbage piles left by campaigning soldiers. Roman writings mention pepper in the context of its medicinal uses but also make it clear that cooks increasingly used it to flavor food. A second century cookbook containing 468 recipes lists pepper as an ingredient in 349 of them. Pepper, to say nothing of salt, was a much-sought spice for meat, both to preserve it for later use and to make it taste better. Romans also added pepper to vegetables, wine, and desserts.

Though cheaper than Indian or Sri Lankan cinnamon or Chinese ginger, pepper remained pricey enough to be an acceptable gift. Nonetheless, as its popularity spread it became a sort of status symbol, an item brought out to impress others, as well as a genuine addition to Roman cuisine.

Other Indian products carried even higher prestige and price tags. The various cinnamon oils, for example, cost ten to hundreds of times more than black pepper. The emperor Nero, out of love and extravagance, burned a year's supply of cinnamon at his wife's funeral. But cinnamon had everyday uses, albeit everyday to Romans with money.

It was a popular ingredient in perfume, indicative of cinnamon's connection to Roman ideas of love. The gods of the ancient Greek stories beloved by the Romans always seemed to appear smelling of perfume. Paris promised Helen that the Trojans would burn cinnamon in her honor if she accompanied him to Troy. She did. The Roman writer Apulius specifically dabbed Venus, the goddess of love, in Arabian scents. In the same story Cupid's hair was said to smell of cinnamon. Romans of both sexes, inspired by such stories, applied a little cinnamon—or a lot—in search of love.

Incense used in religious services contained cinnamon and pepper, among many other spices, herbs, and good-smelling plant resins. Ancient peoples, Roman and otherwise, sprinkled the ingredients into animal fat for burning. Cinnamon sticks could also be thrown straight into a fire. People burned incense at the statues

A bronze (first century BCE) of Venus, the goddess of love, loosening her sandal

of gods and heroes. Roman sailors, like Greek sailors before them, took handheld incense burners onto their ships to appease the gods and guarantee a safe voyage. The devout offered spice-scented incense to household gods every morning and at the same time made their homes smell better.

Gold for Pepper

Tremendous amounts of Roman gold and silver went east to pay for Indian goods. That thousands of Roman coins sit in Indian museums today attests to the shift in wealth. India's Archaeology Department claims 100,000 coins came from just the delta of the Cauvery River, one of the stops for spice ships.

Gold coin of Justinian, excavated in south India

Government leaders declared the loss of money a crisis at least as early as 22 CE, when Tiberius, the emperor, equated buying Asian imports with subversion against Rome. Later that century, the always quotable Pliny complained about how pepper was draining the empire of its treasure. He could not understand the spice's appeal. "Neither the berry nor the fruit of pepper has anything to recommend it," he said. Writers of the time often used pepper as an example when mocking Roman greed or love of the good life.

Roman coins unearthed in India date to as late as the 400s. But the majority was minted in the first two centuries CE, suggesting the Rome-India trade peaked during that period. After the early 200s, Rome had more and more trouble defending the eastern areas of its empire. Acquiring spices became more dangerous. Less supply soon led to higher prices. Pepper, though never exactly common, reverted to being a luxury.

Invasions by peoples like the Visigoths and Huns shook Italy in the 400s. We know because in 408 the Visigoth king Alaric camped outside Rome and demanded 3,000 pounds of pepper—as well as gold, silver, silk, and scarlet hides—to spare the city. Forty-one years later the Romans bribed Attila the Hun with pepper and Indian jewels.

As Rome declined, Arab merchants took back control of the seaborne spice trade. Byzantine (Greek) and Jewish traders handled much of the overland product that ended up in Europe. Pepper, costus, cinnamon, and cardamom, as well as non-Indian spices like clove and ginger, show up—albeit on rare occasions—in European writings of the fifth through eighth centuries. We know Byzantine ships made an annual run to India in addition to trading via the Silk Roads.

New Operators

In 632, the prophet Muhammad, founder of the Islamic religion and a former Arab merchant, finished uniting most of Arabia under one government. Though he died that year, Muhammad's new faith, carried by irresistible Arab armies, began an explosive spread across the middle of Eurasia. Just 120 years later, Muslims had conquered an empire that stretched from modern-day Spain in the west, through North Africa and the Middle East, to Central Asia and beyond the Indus River.

Muslim navies, at the same time, controlled the Indian Ocean. Arab businessmen set up shop in Sri Lanka. That they also kept warehouses on the Malabar Coast is possible. Whatever the case, it's clear they found Indians willing to do business. Both sides benefitted. India's merchants found new partners—better still, a partner that would in time revive and then expand the spice trade beyond the levels it had enjoyed in Roman times. Muslims, mostly forbidden to trade with Christians in Europe, could make their livings, even their fortunes, dealing with Hindus, Buddhists, and Jains.

The Sack of Rome by the Barbarians in 410, an 1890 oil painting by Joseph-Noël Sylvestre

Friendly trade with India allowed Muslims to tap new products and, eventually, new lands. Indian merchants had become players in trade with China, Java, Sumatra, and the mysterious Spice Islands—the last the sole sources of nutmeg and clove, two of the most rare and wildly expensive products of the Middle Ages. Muslim traders acquired these goods and many others from Indian middlemen for sale. Alexandria, recast as a Muslim city, retained its status as a trading center for Indian products.

As the medieval era continued, spices became rare in non-Muslim Europe. Pepper's value there made it the centerpiece of gifts to nobles and foreign kings. Monks traded cinnamon and pepper to monarchs and bishops for favors. Serfs paid in pepper for their freedom. For centuries most Europeans had no access to spices, though that changed in the later part of the medieval era. But they still associated those rare tastes with India, an India that had ceased to be a real place to them and had become, in their imaginations, a land of strange beasts and peoples, of riches and fantastic legends.

The Malabar Coast remained essential as a source of pepper and other spices. But Hindu merchants began to retreat.

As the centuries of the Common Era passed, the Brahmin class increasingly pressed Hindus to avoid Yavana—and all lower caste persons, regardless of nationality—to avoid being "contaminated" by their presence. Such restrictions made trade next to impossible.

Buddhists and Jains, rejecting caste distinctions, could deal with Yavana and anyone else. Trade, in fact, was already a popular occupation within the Buddhist community. But Muslims, for the most part, took the Hindus' place in Asia's trade. In the process they exported Islam to Indonesia and even the distant Philippines. Still, India remained a stop on the Muslim sea trade routes, as well as those of other Asian nations, and the Malabar Coast would long supply pepper and the other spices for which it was famous. It continues to do so today.

The European Arrival

In the 1420s, Prince Henry (the Navigator) of Portugal spearheaded an effort to explore, and exploit, Africa's western coast. Using a new speedy and lightweight ship called the caravel, Portuguese captains steadily inched south, discovering the Azores and soon passing Cape Bojador, heretofore considered the edge of the known world. After Henry's death a private company continued the program. In the 1470s Portuguese ships were trading with Africans for gold and slaves in the Gulf of Guinea.

The Discovery Monument in Lisbon, Portugal. Built in 1960, the monument celebrates Portuguese navigators and the discovery of the New World. Henry the Navigator takes place of pride at the front of the monument.

Portugal's rulers, like most monarchs, needed money. Trade in the Gulf of Guinea was one thing. But India offered true riches. Alas for the Portuguese, Venice controlled Europe's piece of the overland spice trade. Muslims continued to dominate—and profit hugely from—the routes that passed through the Middle East. Opening a new Indian Ocean route to the east was the only real option if Portugal wanted trade with Asia.

Caravels continued to probe southward in hopes of finding a way into the Indian Ocean. In March, 1478, Bartolomeu Dias took a pair of ships around the southern tip of Africa. Dias's crews refused to sail on to India despite their captain's desire to do so. But he returned to Lisbon with the news he had found the way to the Indian Ocean.

It took Portugal time to capitalize on the information. Spain, in the meantime, bet on a route west, across the Atlantic Ocean, to India. Spain and Portugal edged toward war over their (still nonexistent) spice trades. The 1494 Treaty of Tordesillas, however, divided the Atlantic between the two countries, with Portugal getting areas east of an imaginary line, and therefore the sea route around Africa.

The Portuguese soldier-explorer Vasco da Gama departed Lisbon on July 8, 1497. He commanded about 170 men aboard four ships armed with cannons. On board were the most up-to-date maps and advanced navigational tools. Dias piloted for the expedition on the first leg of the journey.

Reaching the Cape of Good Hope, da Gama burned one unneeded ship and turned north. Soon the Portuguese entered the Muslim trade network. Close escapes and the looting of Arab merchant ships followed. An Indian Ocean pilot joined da Gama during a stop at an African port and guided the Portuguese into friendly monsoon winds. Da Gama's fleet crossed the Indian Ocean in less than a month.

On May 20, 1498, the people of Calicut—those paying attention, anyway—watched the Portuguese ships arrive. Historians have yet to find a record of what local people thought of this ominous new group of Yavana. Da Gama would have a hard time making friends in Calicut. The local Muslim merchants, recognizing competition, undermined his efforts. But he returned to Lisbon a hero.

In the following years, large Portuguese fleets made a once-yearly journey to fill their ships' holds with Indian pepper, cinnamon, and other luxuries. Portuguese guns, and the sailors' willingness to use them, soon established forts on India's mainland and gave Portugal control of much of the shipping going into and out of the Malabar Coast.

Dominance of the spice trade made Portugal a superpower, for a time. But India's pepper and cinnamon also attracted the interest of other European powers.

Hindu and Muslim kingdoms maintained considerable, though diminishing, power and influence in India over the next three centuries. Da Gama, however, had opened up India to foreign domination. Portugal, France, the Netherlands, and Great Britain spent centuries fighting for India's riches. Britain eventually conquered much of India itself.

India would absorb these outside influences, as it had going back to the Arya, while also being changed by them. But it would never be the same.

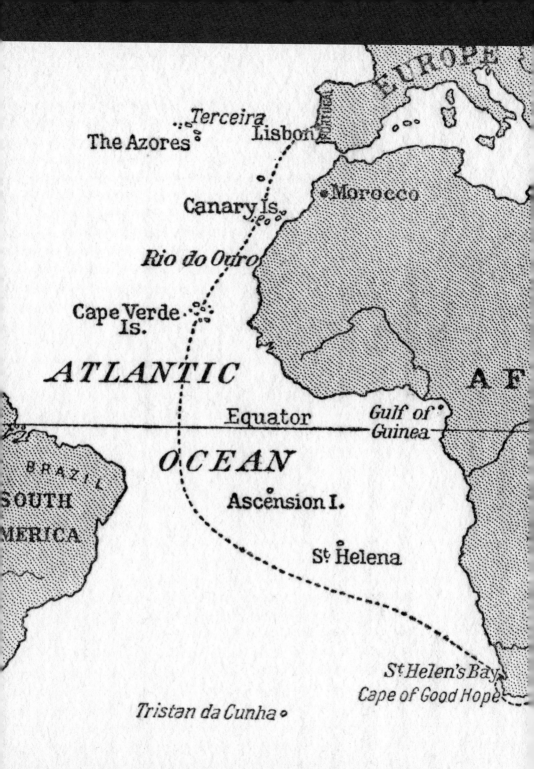

A map illustrating Vasco da Gama's voyages. The dotted line indicates the first voyage to India in 1497.

The Rediscovery of Muziris?

Roman accounts mentioned Muziris (Muciri in Tamil), a Malabar Coast city. Roman ships, pushed by the monsoon, typically put in to Muziris around September and left in December or January, depending on when the winds shifted. Archaeologist Federico Romanis valued the goods on a single Roman ship at 68,000 pieces of gold. Historians assume any city capable of handling such volume in trade was good-sized and well-populated.

Yet at some point after those Romans wrote about Muziris, the city disappeared.

Its location became one of the mysteries of Indian archaeology. The presumed location, based in part on an 1887 book written by a British government official, put Muziris somewhere around Kodungallur, the former capital of a Hindu dynasty that today sits near Kochi (formerly Cochin), itself a major spice trade destination. Archaeological digs in 1945 and 1969 failed to support the official's theory, though.

Studies of the coastline found evidence that the course of the Periyar River had changed. Since the Romans placed Muziris on the river's northern bank, the waterway's location in ancient times was an important piece of information.

One of the researchers, Shajan Paul, soon learned of an ancient brick wall unearthed by accident in Pattanam, a nearby town. In 1983, Pattanam had made news when a stash of Roman coins was discovered. Since Paul theorized that the Periyar might have flowed near Pattanam before its shift, the town seemed an intriguing possible alternative location for Muziris.

It took six years for an archaeological team to come together to dig at Pattanam. Two three-meter-deep pits yielded Roman artifacts. A second expedition in 2007 turned up a wharf with a small boat dated to the first century BCE. The workers also found pepper, cardamom, and other plant remains. Shajan and fellow archaeologist V. Selvakumar learned that locals had been finding glass beads and pieces of Mediterranean pottery for years. Heavy rain, it seemed, soaked the ground and brought objects to the surface.

Archaeologists, often cautious, have yet to declare they have finally found Muziris. Digs continue at Pattanam to find enough evidence to make or disprove such a claim.

 # Sources

CHAPTER ONE:

Ancient Cities

p. 22,   "Despite extensive excavations . . ." George F. Dales, "The Mythical Massacre at Mohenjo-Daro," *Expedition* 6:3 (Spring 1964), 38.

CHAPTER TWO:

Words Spoken, Words Written

p. 34,   "Krishna, I hanker not . . ." S. Prabhavananda and Frederick Manchester, *The Upanishads: Breath of the Eternal* (Hollywood, CA: Vedanta, 1947), 168.

p. 39,   "On conquering Kalinga . . ." John Keay, *India: A History* (New York: Grove Press, 2010), 91.

p. 41,   "All men are my children . . ." V. S. Dhammika, "The edicts of King Ashoka: An English rendering," http://www.cs.colostate. edu/~malaiya/ashoka.html.

p. 41,   "There is no gift comparable..." Keay, *India: A History*, 94.

CHAPTER THREE:

The Spindle and the Crucible

p. 50,   "a substance called sakkharon . . ." Andrew Dalby, *Dangerous Tastes: The Story of Spices* (Berkeley, CA: University of California Press, 2000), 27.

p. 52,   "He who, having pure body . . ." American Museum of Natural History, exhibit, The Nature of Diamonds, "Hindu interpretations and Indian transformations." http://www.amnh.org/exhibitions/diamonds/ hindu.html.

CHAPTER FOUR:

Indian Medicine

p. 65,   "Everyone admires a . . ." Roy Porter, *The Greatest Benefit to Mankind* (New York: Norton, 1997), 139.

p. 68,   "The art of making . . ." K. K. Bhishagratna, translator, *The Sushruta Samhita* (Calcutta: Wilkins Press, 1907), 71–72.

CHAPTER FIVE:

Spices of Life

p. 82,   "[The Arabs] cut all . . ." Herodotus, *The Persian Wars,* George Rawlinson, translator (New York: Modern Library, 1942), 266–267.

p. 89,   "Neither the berry . . ." Tom Standage, *An Edible History of Humanity* (New York: Walker and Company, 2009), 73.

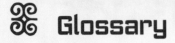 # Glossary

Ayurveda
The system of traditional Indian medicine, Ayurveda dates to ancient times. Its core concepts are laid out in a pair of texts, the *Caraka Samhita* and the *Sushruta Samhita*.

Brahmi
Brahmi refers to the early system of writing used in India.

Brahmin
A Brahmin is a person born into the elite priestly caste in India's caste system. Descended from the Arya elite, the Brahmins later dominated not only the priesthood but the ruling classes. In ancient times Brahmin was a title given to someone who had great knowledge of spiritual matters, regardless of birth.

Buddhism
A religious and philosophical system, Buddhism is usually dated for the fifth century BCE. It arose in part as a rejection of the Brahmin religion. Buddhism's complex beliefs include living according to the teachings of its founder, the Buddha, and seeking escape from the cycle of reincarnation (a state known as nirvana).

Caste system
India's caste system divided different classes of people into four groups: priests, warriors, merchants, and servants. Those outside the caste system, were considered "untouchables."

dharma
A system of ethical behavior based on the teachings of the Buddha.

Hinduism
India's most ancient and dominant religion, Hinduism is not a single faith but an umbrella term that includes many related religious/philosophical systems drawing on knowledge from the Vedas and other ancient Sanskrit texts. Practices, beliefs, and even the concept of God can vary from sect to sect.

Indus Valley Civilization
Also called the Harappan civilization after one of its largest cities, the Indus Valley Civilization took root along the Indus River sometime around 3300 BCE. It began to decline after 1900 BCE and vanished about two hundred years later.

Islam
Originating in Arabia, Islam was founded in the early part of the 600s by the Arab prophet Muhammad. Its followers are called Muslims.

medieval
The medieval period, sometimes called the Middle Ages, refers to the historical period between 400 and 1400.

Glossary continued

monsoon
In premodern times, monsoon meant the system of sea winds in the Indian Ocean. Monsoon winds more or less reliably blew from the southwest part of the year and then switched to drier, more moderate northeast winds.

Periplus
The *Periplus* was a Greek-language guide, author unknown, describing the trade routes linking the Roman Empire to India and Africa. The author's description of the monsoon revolutionized Roman trade with India.

Prakrit
The Prakrits are a group of languages that evolved as the languages of everyday speech among the non-Sanskrit speaking elite in northern India.

Sanskrit
Sanskrit is an ancient language possibly brought to India by the Arya. Its earliest known use is in the oldest parts of the *Rig Veda*. By the early years of the Common Era, Sanskrit had ceased to be a spoken language outside of certain religious and intellectual settings.

Silk Roads
The Silk Roads were a network of trade routes that in premodern times connected East Asia with South and Central Asia, the Middle East, North and East Africa, and Europe. Historians sometimes include the sea routes running from China through the Indian Ocean to points west as part of the Silk Roads network.

standardization
Standardization is a process that imposes agreed to rules, or standards, on the quality, size, or other aspects of technology, products, behaviors, etc.

Vedas
The Vedas are four Sanskrit sacred texts composed after 1500 BCE. Originally oral documents, the Vedas were taught by one generation to the next for centuries, with the strictest attention paid to making no changes. The *Rig Veda* is the oldest of the texts. The others are the *Yajur Veda*, the *Sama Veda*, and the *Atharva Veda*. Veda means knowledge in Sanskrit.

wootz
Wootz was an early type of steel manufactured in ancient India by mixing semi-melted iron with carbon. Harder than other steel of its time, wootz was much in demand for making weapons and armor.

Yavana
Indians used the term *Yavana*—a corruption of Ionian (Greek)—to refer to foreigners of all kinds. Alternate spellings include *Yunani*, *Unani*, and *Yona*.

✪ Bibliography

Books

Ackerknecht, Erwin H. *A Short History of Medicine*. Baltimore: Johns Hopkins University Press, 1982.

Bhishagratna K. K., trans. *The Sushruta Samhita*. Calcutta: Wilkins Press, 1907.

Bussagli, Mario, and Calembus Sivaramamurti. *5000 Years of the Art of India*. New York: Abrams, 1971.

Chaurasia, Radhey Shyam. *History of Ancient India*. New Delhi: Atlantic, 2008.

Crone, Patricia. *Meccan Trade and the Rise of Islam*. Piscataway, NJ: Gorgias Press, 2004.

Czarra, Fred. *Spices: A Global History*. London: Reaktion Books, 2009.

Dalby, Andrew. *Dangerous Tastes: The Story of Spices*. Berkeley, CA: University of California Press, 2000.

———. *Food in the Ancient World from A to Z*. New York: Routledge, 2003.

Freedman, Paul. *Out of the East: Spices and the Medieval Imagination*. Yale University Press, 2008.

Goodall, Dominic, ed. *Hindu Scriptures*. Berkeley, CA: University of California Press, 1996.

Herodotus. *The Persian Wars*. Translated by George Rawlinson. New York: Modern Library, 1942.

Hershey, J. Willard. *The Book of Diamonds*. New York: Hearthside Press, 1940.

Keay, John. *India: A History*. New York: Grove Press, 2010.

———. *The Spice Route: A History*. Berkeley: University of California Press, 2007.

Bibliography continued

Polo, Marco. *The Customs of the Kingdoms of India.* New York: Penguin, 2007.

Porter, Roy. *The Greatest Benefit to Mankind.* New York: Norton, 1997.

Prabhavananda, S., and Frederick Manchester. *The Upanishads: Breath of the Eternal.* Hollywood, CA: Vedanta, 1947.

Sen, Sailendra Nath, *Ancient Indian History and Civilization, Second Edition.* New Delhi: New Age International, 1999.

Shenk, David. *The Immortal Game.* New York: Random House, 2006.

Smith, C. Wayne, and J. Tom Cothren, eds. *Cotton: Origin, History, Technology, and Production.* New York: Wiley, 1999.

Srivastava, V. C., and Lallanji Gopal, eds. *History of Agriculture in India up to c.1200 A.D.* New Delhi: Centre for Studies in Civilizations, 2008.

Standage, Tom. *An Edible History of Humanity.* New York: Walker and Company, 2009.

Turner, Jack. *Spice: The History of a Temptation.* New York: Knopf, 2004.

Yafa, Stephen. *Big Cotton.* New York: Viking, 2005.

Zimmerman, Leo M., and Ilza Veith. *Great Ideas in the History of Surgery.* San Francisco: Norman, 1993.

Periodicals

Dales, George F. "The Mythical Massacre at Mohenjo-Daro." *Expedition* 6:3 (Spring 1964): 36–43.

Patel, Samir S. "India's underground water temples." *Archaeology* 64:3 (May-June 2011): 36–39.

Rana, R. E., and B. S. Arora. "History of plastic surgery in India." *Journal of Postgraduate Medicine* 48:1 (2002): 76–78.

 # Online

Boyle, Wickham. "India and the history of cotton." *HandEye*. July 29, 2010. http://handeyemagazine.com/content/india-and-history-cotton.

British Broadcasting Corporation. "Chinese made first use of diamond." May 17, 2005. http://news.bbc.co.uk/2/hi/science/nature/4555235.stm.

———. "Search for India's ancient city." June 11, 2006. http://news.bbc.co.uk/2/hi/4970452.stm.

Bunney, Sarah. "Zinc Smelting Began in India." *New Scientist*, December 8, 1983. http://books.google.com/books.

Craddock, Paul. "How zinc was smelted in ancient India." *New Scientist*, March 29, 1984. http://books.google.com/books.

Dhammika, V. S.. "The edicts of King Ashoka: An English rendering." http://www.cs.colostate.edu/~malaiya/ashoka.html.

Gorelick, Leonard, and A. John Gwinett. "Diamonds from India to Rome and beyond." Abstract. *American Journal of Archaeology* 92:4 (October 1988): 547–552. http://www.jstor.org/discover/10.2307/505249.

Kenoyer, Jonathan Mark. "Mohenjo-daro: An Ancient Indus Valley metropolis." Mohenjodaro.net. http://www.mohenjodaro.net/mohenjodaroessay.html.

Kew Gardens, Plant Cultures: Black Pepper. http://www.kew.org/plant-cultures/plants/black_pepper_history.html.

———. Cardamom. http://www.kew.org/plant-cultures/plants/cardamom_landing.html.

———. Cotton. http://www.kew.org/plant-cultures/plants/cotton_landing.html.

———. Ginger. http://www.kew.org/plant-cultures/plants/ginger_landing.html.

———. Indigo. http://www.kew.org/plant-cultures/plants/indigo_history.html.

———. Sugarcane. http://www.kew.org/plant-cultures/plants/sugar_cane_landing.html.

Online continued

Lapham's Quarterly. "Food chains: tomatoes, black pepper, and coffee through the years." July 11, 2011. http://www.huffingtonpost.com/2011/07/11/tomatoes-black-pepper-coffee_n_893475.html.

Louise M. Darling Biomedical Library, exhibit. Spices: Exotic Flavors and Medicines. Undated.

————. Black pepper. http://unitproj.library.ucla.edu/biomed/spice/index.cfm?displayID=20.

————. Cardamom. http://unitproj.library.ucla.edu/biomed/spice/index.cfm?displayID=3.

————. Cassia. http://unitproj.library.ucla.edu/biomed/spice/index.cfm?displayID=6.

————. Cinnamon. http://unitproj.library.ucla.edu/biomed/spice/index.cfm?displayID=5.

————. Ginger. http://unitproj.library.ucla.edu/biomed/spice/index.cfm?displayID=15.

————. Sugar. http://unitproj.library.ucla.edu/biomed/spice/index.cfm?displayID=23.

Mundigler, Chris. "The Spice Trade, Part One: The Ancient Near East." *Labyrinth*, issue 82. Undated. http://www.classics.uwaterloo.ca/labyrinth_old/issue82/The%20Ancient%20Spice%20Trade.pdf.

————. "Part Two: Egypt and North Africa." *Labyrinth*, issue 83. Undated. http://www.classics.uwaterloo.ca/labyrinth_old/issue83/83mundigler.htm.

————. "Part Three: Greece and Rome." *Labyrinth*, issue 85. Undated. http://www.classics.uwaterloo.ca/labyrinth_old/issue85/The%20Ancient%20Spice%20Trade.pdf.

————. "Part Four: Rome and the Early Middle Ages." *Labyrinth*, issue 85. Undated. http://www.classics.uwaterloo.ca/labyrinth_old/issue85/The%20Ancient%20Spice%20Trad1.pdf.

Raghu Nandan, K. R. "Zinc metallurgy in ancient India." *Deccan Herald*. August 7, 2007. http://inae.org/metallurgy/News_pdf%20files/DH_07_08_07.pdf.

Raja, M. "India's ancient spice trade gets a makeover." *Asia Times Online*. September18, 2007. http://www.atimes.com/atimes/South_Asia/II18Df01.html.

Ray, Aniruddha. "Indian technology down the ages." *The Hindu*. August 13, 2009. http://www.thehindu.com/arts/books/article2312.ece.

Roach, John. "Faceless Indus Valley city puzzles archaeologists." *National Geographic Online*. Undated. http://science. nationalgeographic.com/science/archaeology/mohenjo-daro/.

Sanderson, Katherine. "Sharpest cut from nanotube sword." *Nature Online*. November 15, 2006. http://www.nature.com/news/2006/061113/full/news061113-11.html.

Saraf, Sanjay. "Sushruta: Rhinoplasty in 600 B.C." *The Internet Journal of Plastic Surgery* 3:2 (2007). http://www.ispub.com/journal/the-internet-journal-of-plastic-surgery/volume-3-number-2/sushruta-rhinoplasty-in-600-b-c.html.

Sperati, G. "Amputation of the nose throughout history." Reprinted via Pubmed from *Acta Otorhinolaryngol Ital.* 29 (1) (February 2009): 44–50. http://www.ncbi.nlm.nih.gov/pmc/articles/PMC2689568/.

Srivathsan, A. "In search of Muziris." *The Hindu*. May 1, 2010. http://www.thehindu.com/arts/magazine/article418904.ece.

Times of India. "Ancient glass-making furnace discovered." *Times of India*. June 22, 2009. http://articles.timesofindia.indiatimes.com/2009-06-22/chennai/28152601_1_beads-glass-making-ancient-trade-route.

———. "IIT team solves the pillar mystery." *Times of India*. March 21, 2005. http://articles.timesofindia.indiatimes.com/2005-03-21/india/27850444_1_corrosion-iron-iit.

van der Veen, Marijke. "Roman and Islamic spice trade." University of Leicester School of Archaeology and Ancient History. Press release. Undated. http://www2.le.ac.uk/departments/archaeology/research/projects/spice.

Verhoeven, J. D., Pendray, A. H., and W. E. Dauksch. "The key role of impurities in ancient Damascus steel blades." *JOM* 50: 9 (1998): 58–64. http://www.tms.org/pubs/journals/jom/9809/verhoeven-9809.html.

Online continued

Viswanath, Rohit. "Ancient India was in the middle of global trade." *Times of India*. June 15, 2007. http://articles.timesofindia.indiatimes.com/2007-06-15/edit-page/27962857_1_silk-route-marine-archaeology-trade.

Wasserman, Tina D. "Cooking: the Spice Trade and the Jews." *Reform Judaism*. Winter 2007. http://reformjudaismmag.org/Articles/index.cfm?id=1299.

Other Media

Public Broadcasting System. "The Story of India."
http://www.pbs.org/thestoryofindia/about/episode_summaries/.

Web sites

American Museum of Natural History, exhibit. The Nature of Diamonds.
http://www.amnh.org/exhibitions/diamonds/index.html.

British Museum: Indus Seal
http://www.britishmuseum.org/explore/highlights/highlight_objects/asia/s/indus_seal.aspx.

Indus Valley Civilization
http://www.harappa.com/har/har0.html.

Louise M. Darling Biomedical Library, exhibit. Spices: Exotic Flavors and Medicines
http://unitproj.library.ucla.edu/biomed/spice/index.cfm.

Index

Index continued

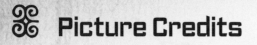

Picture Credits

All images used in this book not in the public domain are credited in the listing that follows:

Cover: Courtesy of Grjatoi
8:        Courtesy of the David Rumsey Historical Map Collection
10–11:   Courtesy of KennyOMG
12–13:   Courtesy of Comrogues from San Francisco, California
16–17:   Top: Courtesy of Raveesh Vyas
20:       Courtesy of Ismoon
26–27:   North Wind Picture Archives/Alamy
31:       Mary Evans Picture Gallery/Alamy
40:       World Religions Photo Gallery/Alamy
50:       Courtesy of Evan Izer
51:       Courtesy of Gitane
54:       Portrait Courtesy of Library of Congress
56–57:   Courtesy Kujit Kumar
60–61:   Courtesy of Digishagautam
68–69:   Fotoflirt Creative/Alamy
71:       Werli Francois/Alamy
75:       Courtesy of Sugeesh
76:       Courtesy of Quadell
77:       Courtesy of Frank C. Müller
80:       Courtesy of Ragesoss
83:       Courtesy of Library of Congress
85:       Courtesy of Koshy Koshy
86:       Tibor Bognar/Alamy
88:       Courtesy Walters Art Museum, Baltimore, Maryland
96–97:   Classic Image/Alamy

P9-CLU-371